BRASSEY'S
Book of
BODY ARMOR

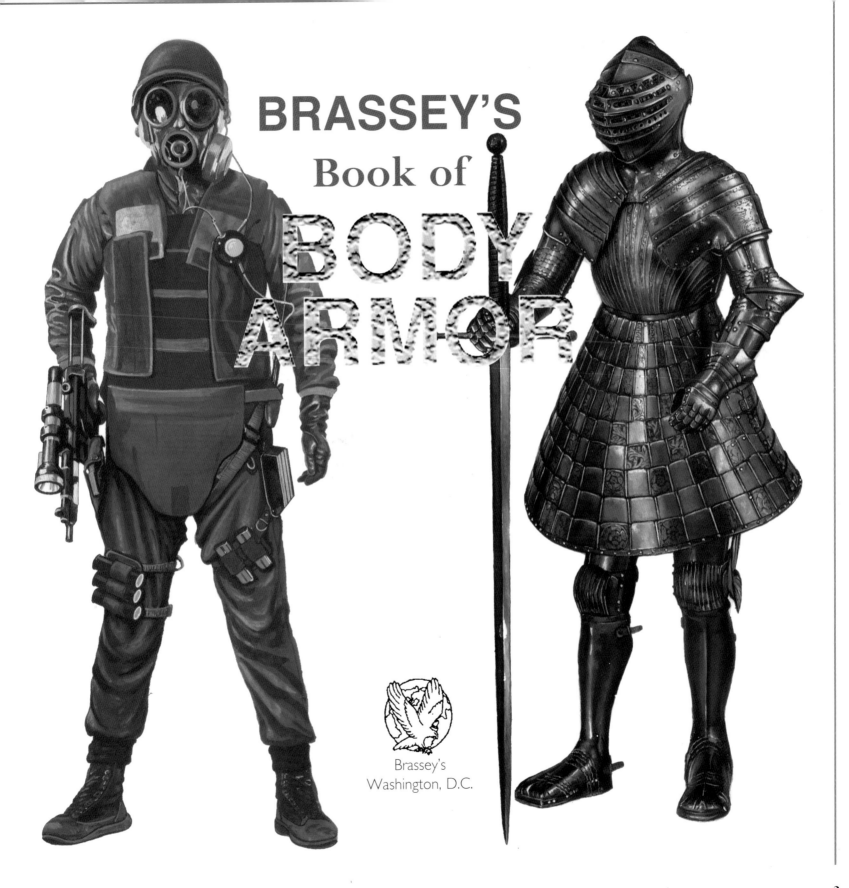

BRASSEY'S
Book of
BODY ARMOR

Brassey's
Washington, D.C.

First published in the United Kingdom by Pegasus Publishing Ltd.

This edition of Brassey's Book of Body Armor published 2001 by Brassey's, 22841 Quicksilver Drive, Dulles, Virginia 20166
© Ray Hutchins, Merlin Publications, 2000.
© Text from page 10 to page 103 -
   Robert Woosnam-Savage 2000.

ISBN 1-57488-293-7 (alk paper)

Printed in Singapore on acid-free paper that meets the American National Standards Institute Z39-48 Standard

Brassey's
22841 Quicksilver Drive
Dulles, Virginia 20166

First Edition

10 9 8 7 6 5 4 3 2 1

Library of Congress Cataloging-in-Publication Data
Brassey's Book of Armor by
Robert Woosnam-Savage and Anthony Hall.

Includes bibliographical references and index.

CREDITS

This book relies upon the work of many experts in the field such as: Blair, Norman, Reid, Robinson, and Yadin. The authors would also like to personally thank Philip Abbott, Ian Bottomley, Stephen Howe, Antonia Lovelace, Guy Wilson, and other colleagues and friends, for their valuable assistance and patience.

Text and captions by:
Robert Woosnam-Savage and Anthony Hall

Illustrations by:
Ray Hutchins, Julian Mason and Graham Bingham

Designed by: Ray Hutchins
Maps drawn by: Ray Hutchins

This book is dedicated to Arthur Gaye, whose original idea, with Ray Hutchins, has at last reached fruition.
It is also dedicated to one perfect Knight - Edward Woosnam-Savage.

CONTENTS

FOREWORD

From the Master of the Armouries

ROYAL ARMOURIES

It is a pleasure to announce the arrival of a new book on the history of armor. It is intended as an introduction to this fascinating subject. It has a short but authoritative text that is complemented by accurate illustrations showing vividly the variety of armored protection humankind has developed and adopted around the world and through the ages.

Human beings are soft-skinned animals with an aggressive streak. From early in our development we have found the need to protect ourselves against the animals we hunt or who hunt us and against others of our own species. First we used the furs, skins, bones and even teeth of other animals to keep us safer. To these were soon added other natural materials, such as wood, and fabrics made from plant and animal material, then came metals. As first bronze and then iron were utilised to make better tools and weapons so the same materials came to be used to protect against these better weapons. But the use of fabrics and soft armor never went entirely out of use, and in recent years, with the advent of made-made fibres of enormous strength, we have come almost full circle.

In every part of the world humans have developed different forms and types of armored protection. This fascinating story is here brought vividly to life.

GM Wilson
<u>Master of the Armouries.</u>

An impression of Norman knights preparing for combat before the Battle of Hastings, October 14, 1066. They are shown wearing mail hauberks and coifs, together with their conical helmets and kite shields.

INTRODUCTION

Whenever body armor is mentioned in connection with military history, it is usually the armors of the knights of medieval Europe, or those of the samurai warriors of Japan that spring to mind. But these are only two amongst numerous types and forms of armor protection that have been developed.

Body Armor is a guide and introduction to the history of some of the armors that have been used by many peoples, in many places. Although admittedly concentrating on developments in the West, the authors hope that the present work will give a broad impression of the history of armor worldwide.

As with many beginnings, the first use of armor is lost in pre-history. Humankind, perhaps the most aggressive of species, differs from others in the animal kingdom, from the crab to the rhino in being soft-bodied. We do not possess a natural outer shell or thick hide to protect us from attack.

Although it is not known where, when, by whom, or against what armor was first used, it was in all probability devised for protection against wild animal attack whilst hunting. It was only a short step then from being a defense against animals to being a defense against an attack from other people. Given the history of conflict through the millennia and the fact that the hunting spear, as a weapon of attack, has been in existence for over 400,000 years, and the bow and arrow for about 30,000 years, the first use of armor protection may have occurred somewhere in between.

An Egyptian tomb painting from Hierakonpolis, dated to the 4th millennium BC, shows men fighting each other, some apparently bearing shields made from animal hide. This scene is probably one of the earliest records of armor in its most basic form: the shield, a hand-held portable defense. For some peoples this form of armor was all that was ever necessary. Until recently Australian aborigines used the tamarang, a wooden parrying shield, to deflect missile weapons such as spears, and blows from clubs. The tamarang may have been altered little during hundreds, if not thousands, of years, but clearly elsewhere technologies have changed dramatically over time. Armors have developed and evolved not just because of the fact that the materials they are made from have become ever more sophisticated, but that the threat itself has become more violent. A tamarang deflects a blow from a club only as powerful as the man wielding it; a body vest today is expected to stop a full-metal-jacketed bullet traveling at over 2,700 feet per second (825 m/sec) driven by the finest propellant modern chemical science can devise. The basic idea of armor may be considered almost timeless: to protect the vulnerable parts of the body; but the armors themselves have had to change as the threat to the individual has changed.

The history of armor also poses the important question: who is worth protecting? The first evidence of manufactured body armor comes from depictions of Sumerian armies and the tombs of their kings and nobles. Such technology was costly, and armor quickly became associated with rank, wealth, and privilege. It became a symbol of power. The man was worth protecting because he had the rank and wealth to afford it. It wasn't until the 20th century that armor truly became democratized. Conscript citizen armies were put into battle across continents and came to expect at least a steel helmet to wear. These may have been armors of the production line, turned out in their millions, but as symbols they became just as powerful.

We hope that this book prompts the interested reader to delve deeper into the subject. To facilitate this a listing of where to see some of the finest collections of armor in the world, together with an extended select bibliography, is included.

The topic of armor is still very relevant today. Despite the amazing technological changes in recent decades, it is sadly true that there is probably more conflict, and so more armor being used today, than at any other time.

Robert Woosnam-Savage and Anthony Hall
October, 2000

Detail from a wall painting from an Egyptian tomb at Hierakonpolis (4th millennium BC). One of the combatants carries a shield.

WHAT IS ARMOR ?

Right: Details of armor construction:
i) Mail armor with butted rings.
ii) Mail armor with riveted rings.
iii) Mail armor with mixed whole and riveted rings in alternate rows.
iv) Single riveted ring.
v) Single butted ring.

Far Right: Detail of lamellar armor

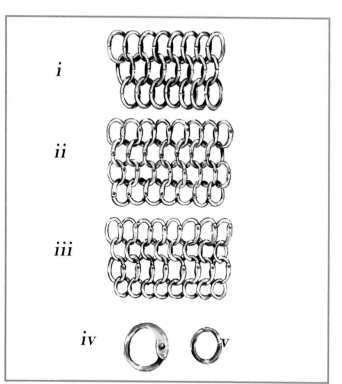

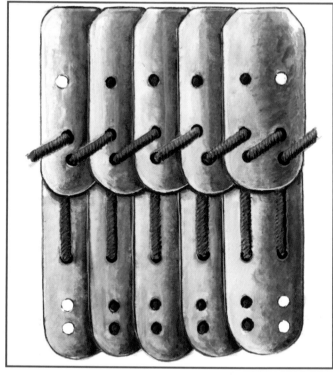

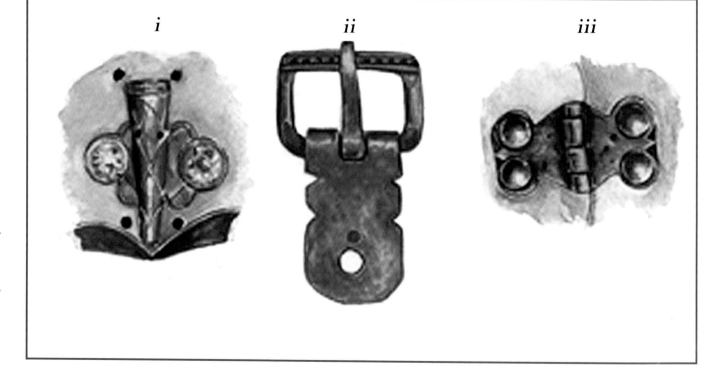

Details of armor construction:
i) Plume holder, mid-16th century AD.
ii) Brass buckle, mid-16th century AD.
iii) Hinge, mid-15th century AD.

Armor can be defined as defensive material made to withstand attack. There are a number of different categories of armor. It can be "soft," made from animal skins or layers of fabric, or "hard," made from plates of horn, hardened leather, wood, or metal. Forms of hard armor include mail (which is made up of small interlinked individual rings of metal, riveted or butted together) and plate armor (made up of large plates attached to each other by straps known as leathers). There is also scale armor (made up of small plates attached to a fabric backing) and lamellar armor (made up of small narrow plates laced together, to create a series of overlapping rows). Lamellar armor evolved from scale armor. Generally speaking, armor worn directly on the body, such as a helmet or breastplate, is usually called "armor." Armor also includes defensive pieces that are carried, namely shields.

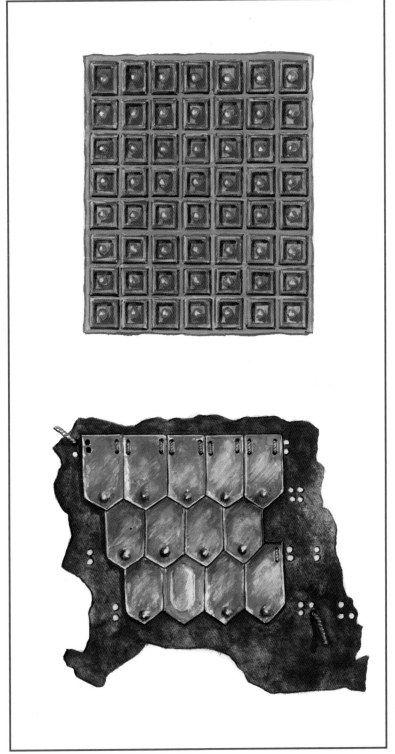

Details of armor construction showing small plates on fabric.

Scale armor. Bronze scales, with small bosses, attached to fabric, from tomb of Sheshonq, Egypt, 10th century BC.

Detail from a wall painting from the Theban tomb painting of Kenamon (about 1436 - 1411 BC). It depicts a wooden shield covered with cowhide. Shields could also be covered with hide from other animals such as antelope and cheetah.

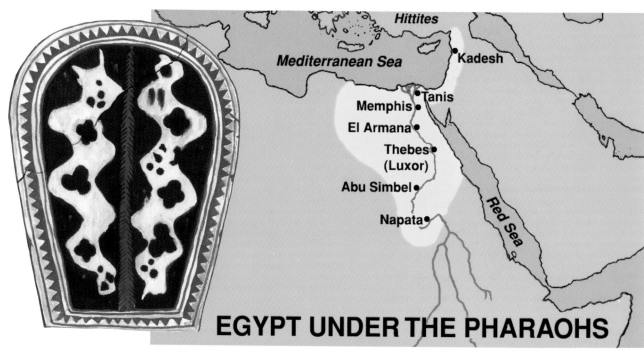

EGYPT UNDER THE PHARAOHS

Egypt - 3000 BC to 1200 BC

By 3100 BC Egypt was united under the warring Pharaoh Menes. There is no evidence of body armor at this time, though large shields of cowhide were used, against the main weapon, the spear. By 2000-1900 BC these shields had become smaller, more rectangular, and had a curved top. Some are shown with what appears to be a small round, probably metal, boss in the upper part. These appear in reliefs depicting forts under siege. Some real shields were found in the tomb of Tutankhamun (reigned 1345- 1335 BC), made of wood overlaid with antelope and cheetah hide. Some Egyptian warriors wore helmets of padded linen, and bronze helmets may also have been worn.

Between 1500-1200 BC scale armor was also used to protect the body. Small plates of bronze were sewn, riveted, or stitched to a leather or padded garment. The earliest representation of scale armor comes from the tomb of Kenamon (from around 1436-1411 BC). A garment of ribbed bronze scales laced to a backing is depicted. Bronze scales of this type of armor have also been found in the palace of Amenhotep III, in Thebes, of 1430 BC. Tuthmosis III (who died about 1450 BC) captured 200 sets of such armor at the battle of Megiddo (1458 BC). A relief of about 1415 BC, from the time of Tuthmosis IV (1470-1400 BC), shows a charioteer wearing scale armor pierced by an arrow. Tutankhamun's tomb also provided a close-fitting sleeveless cuirass made from thick tinted leather scales sewn onto a lining. In a relief in the Ramesseum at Thebes, Rameses II (reigned 1304-1237 BC) is shown fighting at the battle of Kadesh (1275 BC), where he defeated the Hittites. He is depicted wearing a full-length coat of bronze scale armor and a blue helmet-crown. Such armor could be made from over 1,000 separate scales. Not only were individual scales found in the tomb of Rameses III (reigned 1184- 1152 BC), but a wall painting shows scale armor laced together and arranged in rows, like lamellar armor. A fragment of a garment with scales mounted on it survives from the time of the Pharaoh Sheshonq in the 10th century BC.

The infantry wore a cuirass made of padded linen, which sometimes contained scale armor, together with a triangular groin defense.

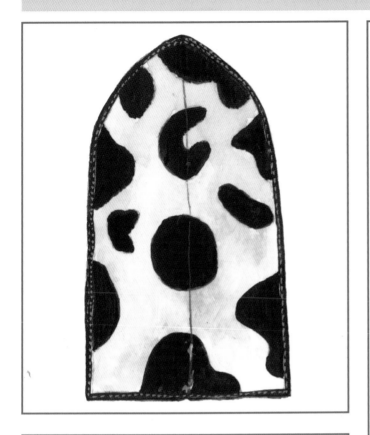

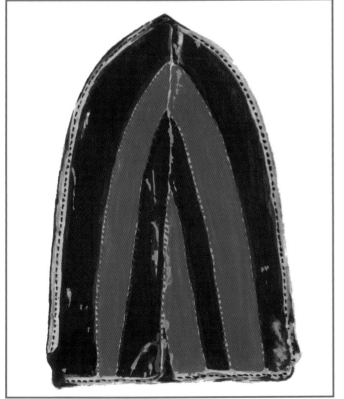

Far Left: Two painted wooden models of Egyptian hide - covered shields (from about 19th-20th centuries BC). They show stitching around the edges and a piebald hide pattern.

Left: Reconstruction of an Egyptian infantryman, from about 19th century BC. He is seen wearing a padded linen cuirass and groin defense. He carries a shield and is armed with a spear and a sickle-shaped sword, a khopesh.

13

Rameses II at the Battle of Kadesh, as depicted in a 13th century BC colored relief in the Ramesseum, Thebes. He is shown wearing a full-length coat of bronze scale armor. As pharaoh he engages in combat, and drives the chariot single-handedly. In reality he would have been accompanied by a charioteer.

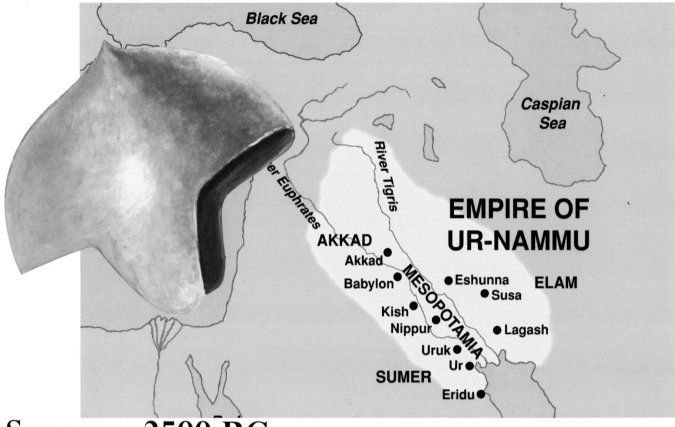

Bronze helmet of the type worn by Sumerian infantrymen, similar to those found in the royal tombs of Ur.

Black Sea

Caspian Sea

River Tigris

River Euphrates

EMPIRE OF
UR-NAMMU

AKKAD

Akkad

Babylon

MESOPOTAMIA

Eshunna

Susa

ELAM

Kish

Nippur

Lagash

Uruk

Ur

SUMER

Eridu

Sumer – 2500 BC

From the city of Sumer in Mesopotamia, during the 3rd millennium BC, comes the first evidence of armor being worn by armies, as well as the first use of four-wheeled waggons as mobile fighting platforms. The so-called Vulture stele (now in the Louvre, Paris) depicts Eannutum, king of the city-state of Lagash about 2500- 2400 BC, in battle, together with his army.

The army was made up of two parts. The light infantry carried spears and long-hafted battle axes. They wore a garment made from something like goat wool, and helmets. As so much early material survives only as images, rather than objects, the details are open to interpretation. It is not possible to determine whether these helmets were made of leather, or a metal, most probably bronze. Bronze, an alloy of tin and copper, was first made around 3500 BC. It can produce a sharper edge than stone,

and was very quickly used to make weapons of attack and defensive armor. The Sumerian heavy infantry wore the same body garment and helmet. They carried spears and also large rectangular shields, probably of animal hide, which covered the body from chin to ankle. On the front of each shield are what appear to be six small raised circular bosses, probably of bronze. The six bosses have been interpreted by scholars as a symbolic reference to six units or six men. In reality each shield probably had only one central boss. It is possible that the spearmen, unable to carry such a large a shield as well as their spears, were accompanied by shield - bearers for protection. The use of long spears and shields suggests they may have fought in phalanx formation, or used shield walls.

Eannutum is shown wearing a helmet closely modeled on what must have been the current hairstyle, including details such as braiding, and the wearing of the hair up at the back, in a bun. Also modeled are the ears. This type of helmet is known to have been of made of metal, as one such helmet has been found. It is made of a single sheet of embossed and chased electrum (an alloy of 15- carat gold and silver), and was therefore probably ceremonial in purpose. It was discovered in the tomb of Meskalam-Dug, a noble of Ur, of about 2500 BC. Reliefs depicting fighting scenes show that the same type of helmet was worn into battle. Most of these battle helmets were probably made of less costly metal, such as bronze or copper.

Similar pieces of armor are shown on the so-called Battle Standard of Ur (now in the British Museum, London), which is a sound box of a lyre from about the same date. Here the infantry are shown wearing long cloaks (probably of animal hide) with what look like metal studs (possibly of bronze). They carry both axes and sickle-shaped swords.

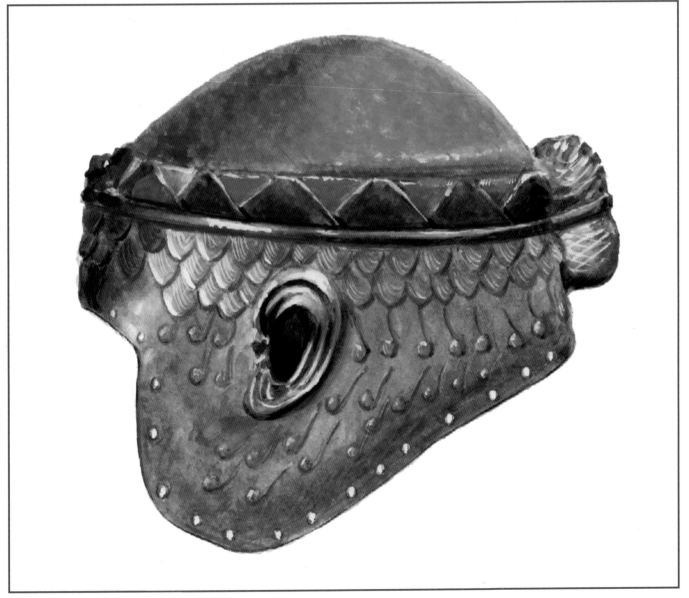

The golden helmet of Meskalam-Dug, of about 2500 BC. It was discovered in the grave of a nobleman of Ur. The holes along its edges were for a lining.

Reconstruction of a Sumerian heavy infantryman, about 2500 BC. His armor consisted of a laced-on helmet and metal-studded cloak. The central boss of his shield may have been made from bronze. It appears that he fought with his spear in a phalanx formation.

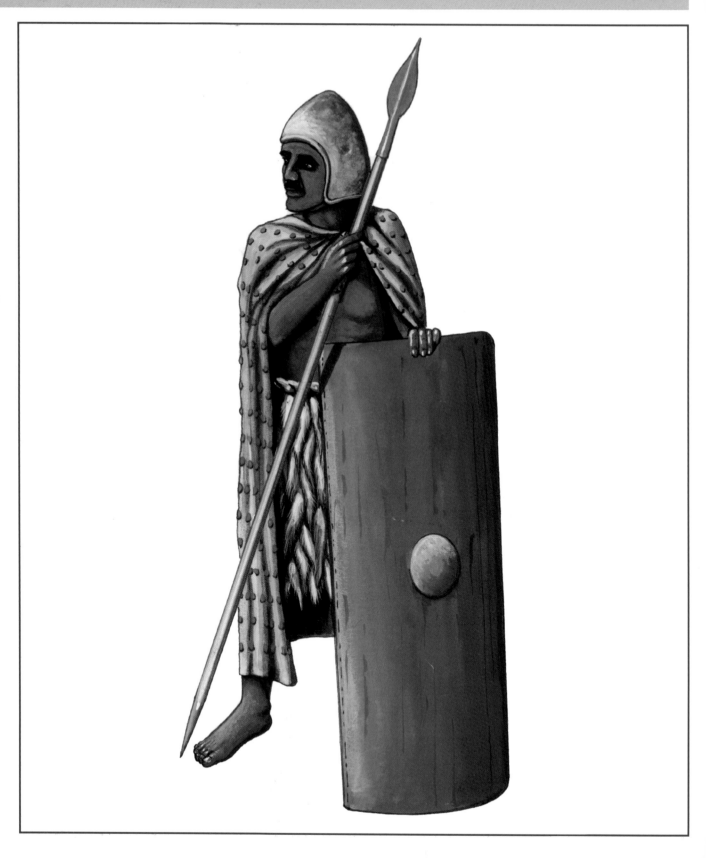

Reconstruction of a Sumerian light infantryman, about 2500 BC. Wearing a helmet, he is armed with a battle-ax and sickle-shaped sword.

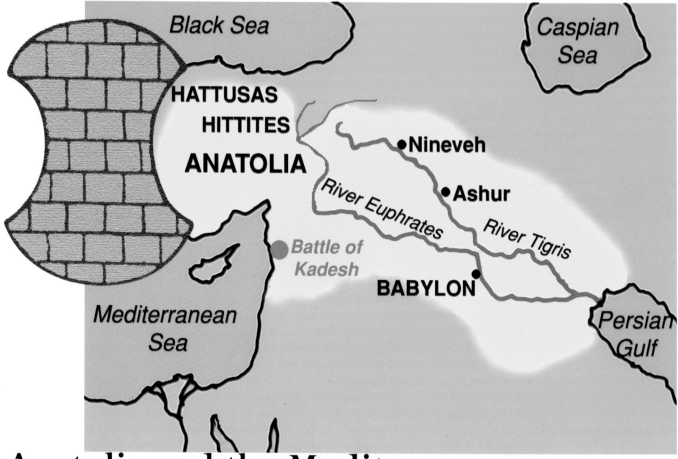

Hittites used shields of different forms including round and small figure-of-eight ones. They were made from wickerwork or wooden-framed with a hide

Anatolia and the Mediterranean – 1500 BC to 1200 BC

The Hittites of Asia Minor controlled an empire between the 14th and 12th centuries BC. From their 18th century kingdom in Anatolia they expanded east and south in the 15th century BC. After their conquest of northern Syria in the 15th century BC the growth of the empire was halted by the Egyptians under Rameses II. The empire disintegrated about 1200 BC under attack from the Assyrians. The Hittites, who seem to have worn scale armor, made helmets of iron from about 1400 BC, some of which appear to have had horns. They developed "figure-of-eight" shaped shields, probably constructed from reeds, and fought with ax and sword, using chariot warfare.

The Sherden, or Shardana, formerly another enemy of Egypt, possibly linked with Sardinia or Cyprus, were one of the "Sea Peoples" that attacked the coastal regions of the eastern Mediterranean early in the 12th century BC. The armor of the Sherden is depicted in various reliefs in Ancient Egypt. They became part of the lifeguard of Rameses II, and participated in the Battle of Kadesh (1275 BC). They are shown carrying round shields and wearing linen armors and horned helmets. The helmets also bear a disc representing Ra, the Sun God. The Sherden used long bronze swords.

Reconstruction of a Sherden warrior of about 1200 BC. He bears a round shield and a laced padded linen cuirass, together with a horned helmet.

Assyrian archers protected by large shields during the attack on Eqron, as depicted in reliefs from the Palace of Sargon, Khorsabad (721- 705 BC).

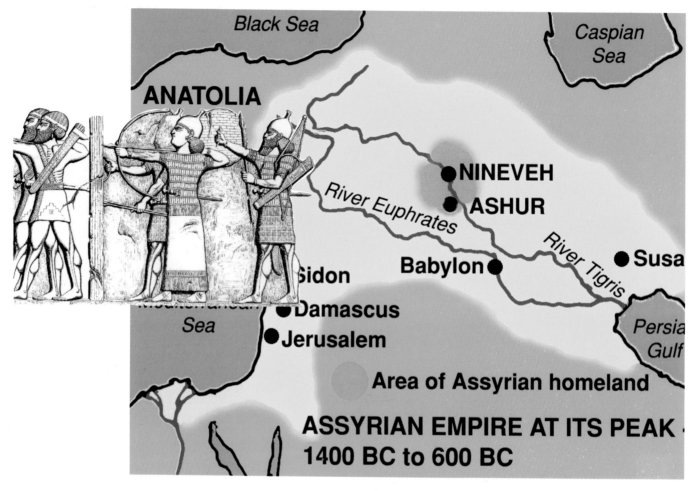

ANATOLIA

Black Sea

Caspian Sea

River Euphrates

● NINEVEH
● ASHUR

River Tigris

Babylon ●

● Susa

Sidon

Mediterranean Sea

● Damascus
● Jerusalem

Persian Gulf

Area of Assyrian homeland

ASSYRIAN EMPIRE AT ITS PEAK 1400 BC to 600 BC

Assyria - 1400 BC to 600 BC

Assyrian reliefs show in great detail the innovative conquering armies of Assyria. The Assyrians appear to have been the first to make wide use of full body armor. It was made up of a cuirass constructed of small bronze plates laced together. This is the first recorded use of the sophisticated form of flexible armor, known as lamellar armor (see pages 10 and 11). By about 700 BC it was worn as an ankle-length defense. Later on, after 1000 BC, the lamellar scales were made of iron, as found in the Assyrian capital of Nimrud, Iraq. Infantry soldiers wore conical bronze helmets with ear defenses. Here also perhaps we have the beginnings of a form of heraldry, as different units were identifiable by the crests of their helmets. They also wore circular pectorals on the center of their chests. They carried either rectangular or circular shields. Other large shields, partially made of reeds, carried by shield-bearers, were used to protect archers who also wore short-sleeved body armors. A later development was a larger shield that could be set upon the ground, from behind which the archer shot. This idea would reappear hundreds of years later in Europe as the European archers' pavise. The larger Assyrian shields were often used when besieging fortified cities, and the Assyrians also employed siege engines, such as battering-rams and siege-towers, and scaling ladders.

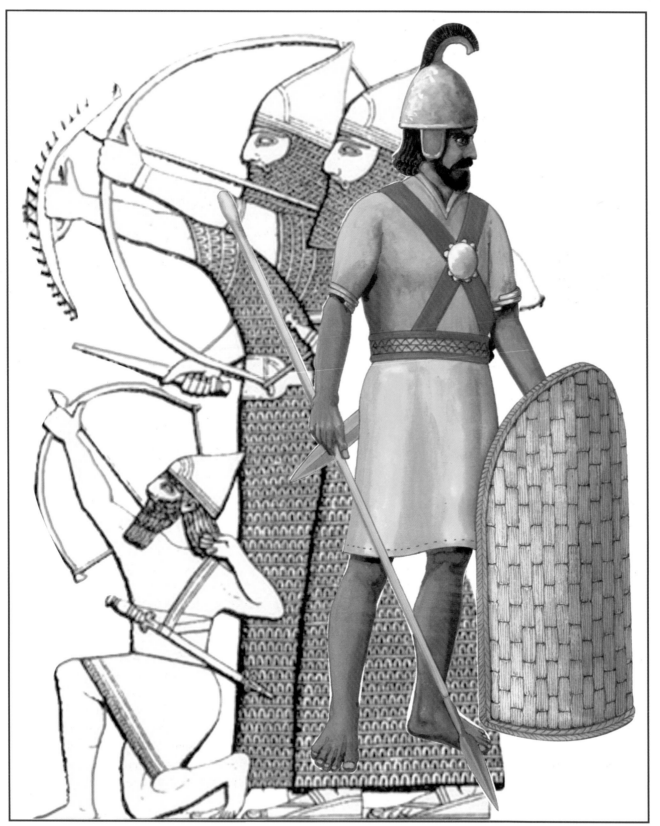

Reconstruction of Assyrian infantryman of the 7th century BC. He wears a helmet and circular pectoral for defense. His shield was made from wickerwork. Behind him archers besieging a city are shown wearing what appears to be a form of lamellar armor. From a relief in the Palace of Ashurnasirpal II, Nimrud (883- 859 BC).

The figure-of-eight shield is the type most commonly depicted in Mycenaean art. It disappeared about 1400 BC, only to reappear in the 8th century BC. It was made from several layers of hide stitched on to a wicker frame.

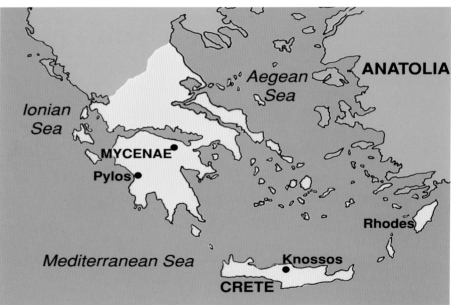

Mycenae: The Armors of the Heroes of Homer – 1400 BC

In 1960 the rock-cut tomb of a warrior was discovered in Midea (present-day Dendra), south of Mycenae, in Greece. The finds inside confirmed details related in the epics of Homer (8th century BC). Plaques of split boar tusks, which would have been attached to a now perished cap, and a bronze cheek-piece were all that was left of a helmet. One is described as being given by Meriones to Odysseus:

"*A leather helmet; the inside of which was stoutly made with many taught interwoven thongs; and which underneath a cap of felt was sewn. Outside the flashing white tusks of boars' gleaming teeth, closely arrayed, facing alternate ways, were well and cunningly set.*"
(Book 10, *The Iliad*, Homer)

It would have taken between 30 and 40 boars to furnish enough tusks to construct such a helmet.

Found with it was an almost complete plate armor, made from large plates of beaten bronze. It consisted of a breast and backplate, a high gorget to protect the throat, two shoulder guards, and three curved plates to protect the lower part of the body and upper leg (the front three shorter than the back set, to allow the wearer more freedom to move). The armor would have been lined with leather, and because of its very heavy weight was probably worn by chariot-borne warriors. Greaves to protect the lower legs were also worn. Homer describes Atreides "*tying round his legs a pair of splendid greaves which were fitted with silver clasps for the ankles.*"
(Book XI, *The Iliad*, Homer)

This armor belonged to a comparatively minor noble. King Agamemnon is described as having had an armor that had "*ten (bands) of dark blue enamel, twelve of gold, and twenty of tin. On either side three snakes rose up in coils toward the opening for the neck.*"
(Book XI, *The Iliad*, Homer)

The Dendra finds demonstrate the amazing level of technical skill that had been achieved in making armor from metal so early on. The ideas and forms differ very little from plate armor solutions in use around AD 1400.

The rectangular shields used by the Mycenaeans, made of hide and wood, were often large. They were described as being "*like a tower, made of bronze and seven layers of leather*"
(Book VII, *The Iliad*, Homer)

Others were of a figure-of-eight shape, similar to those of Crete from the 16th century BC. It is said that when the warrior Hector "*walked, the dark leather rim of his bossed shield tapped him above and below, on the ankles and on the back of his neck.*"
(Book VI, *The Iliad*, Homer)

This also implies that these shields had a neck strap of some kind.

The Dendra panoply. This armor, made up of 15 individual pieces, contains the earliest known bronze cuirass. It was probably worn by a chariot warrior who did not bear a shield.

Two views of a bronze Villanovan crested helmet from central Italy (8th century BC). Such helmets had been in use since about 1300 BC. Over 30 such helmets have been found.

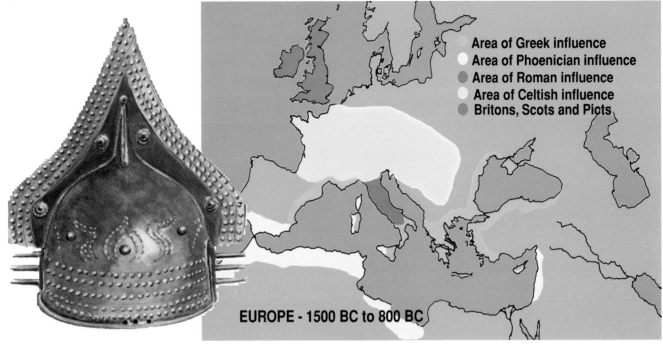

Area of Greek influence
Area of Phoenician influence
Area of Roman influence
Area of Celtish influence
Britons, Scots and Picts

EUROPE - 1500 BC to 800 BC

Europe - 1500 BC to 100 BC

Bronze came into use at different times in different places. In mainland Europe it came later than Greece. However, helmets, cuirasses (with dot and circle decoration), and shields of bronze were soon being manufactured in cultures such as Villanova, northern Italy, and exported widely throughout the Mediterranean. Horned helmets, probably made in Italy, have been found as far north as Viksö, Denmark. The helmets were hammered out of one piece of bronze, or could be made up of two pieces, flanged and riveted together. Flat round shields, with small central bosses and concentric ridges, were backed with leather, to strengthen them.

Mail armor was probably developed by the so-called Celts, perhaps those of Gaul, some time around the 6th or 5th century BC, although the earliest surviving evidence of it is found in a relief sculpture from the Temple of Athene, from Pergamum, Turkey (now in Berlin), of about 160-155 BC. It depicts a trophy of Galatian arms and armor, and includes a mail shirt.

Two views of a helmet, of about 1000–400 BC, which was found in Viksö, in northern Zealand, Denmark. It is made from two sheets of bronze riveted together. The horns are hollow and the front of the helmet bears a grotesque face with a hooked nose.

27

A Greek Corinthian helmet made from bronze (early 5th century BC).

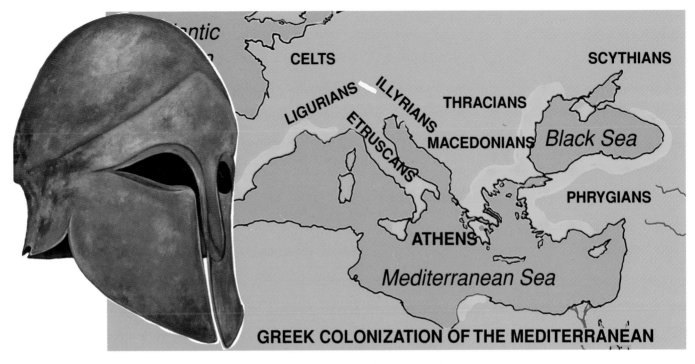

CELTS

SCYTHIANS

LIGURIANS

ILLYRIANS

THRACIANS

ETRUSCANS

MACEDONIANS

Black Sea

PHRYGIANS

ATHENS

Mediterranean Sea

GREEK COLONIZATION OF THE MEDITERRANEAN

Greece – 1000 BC to 300 BC

Greek city states, such as Argos, Athens, Corinth, Sparta, and Thebes, developed alongside new state armies and tactics. The Greek phalanx became the standard fighting formation. It was formed from serried ranks of infantry armed with 10-foot (3-meter) long thrusting spears with long iron spear-heads. They also carried shields and swords. The phalanx was made up of individual soldiers known as hoplites ("shield-bearers"). Units of hoplites would advance, with their long spears thrust forward, toward the enemy. The Greek shield (hoplon) was circular and about 3 feet (1meter) in diameter. It was made of wood and bronze, and was carried by a large arm loop and a leather strap for the hand. Their bronze body armor consisted of helmets, breast - and backplates, or a cuirass of leather or multi-layered linen. The "bell" or "muscled" breastplates were often embossed so as to represent the musculature of the chest and abdomen, and appeared about the 5th century BC. The lower leg was protected by bronze shin defenses, greaves,

Greek chaffron made of bronze, worn on the front of the horse's head (end of 6th century BC).

which do not appear to have been strapped on, but were held in place by the spring of the metal itself (although Homer, presumably describing armor of nearer his own time, does describe greaves that were buckled on). In the 6th century BC separate defenses were also available for the upper arms and the thighs. Greek helmet design included some of the most functional designs, as well as some of the most aesthetically pleasing. The Corinthian style, which protected the head and neck of the wearer, appeared about 700 BC and was made from one piece of

bronze. It had a characteristic "T"-shaped facial opening and nasal bar, protecting the nose. Helmets were lined for comfort, but when not in use they often worn tilted back over the head.

Some Greek warriors found these helmets restricted both their hearing and sight, which in battle could obviously prove fatal. So by the second half of the 4th century BC another form of helmet, the Boeotian, was developed. It was more open-faced, with a large brim, and was also worn by cavalry.

A Greek Boeotian helmet made from bronze (4th century BC). This form of helmet was recommended for cavalrymen because of its good all-round vision.

Scythia - 700 BC to 200 BC

Sometime before the 7th century a nomadic Iranian-speaking tribe of the Western Steppe, called Scythians by the Greeks, began to create a territory that stretched from north of the Black Sea to Mesopotamia. Their cavalry used hit-and-run tactics. Successful long-distance raids included the sacking of the Assyrian capital Nineveh in 612 BC.

The army was made up of freemen, many of whom were horse soldiers. A 5th-century BC Greek historian described them as *"all archers on horseback"* They fought with re-curved double bows, sometimes using poisoned arrows, as well as swords of Persian style and various forms of shield.

Greek-like armor and helmets were worn, and from their tombs it is known that they also wore pectorals to protect the chest. By the 4th century BC they were using scale armor cuirasses.

A Scytho-Iranian pectoral worn on the chest.

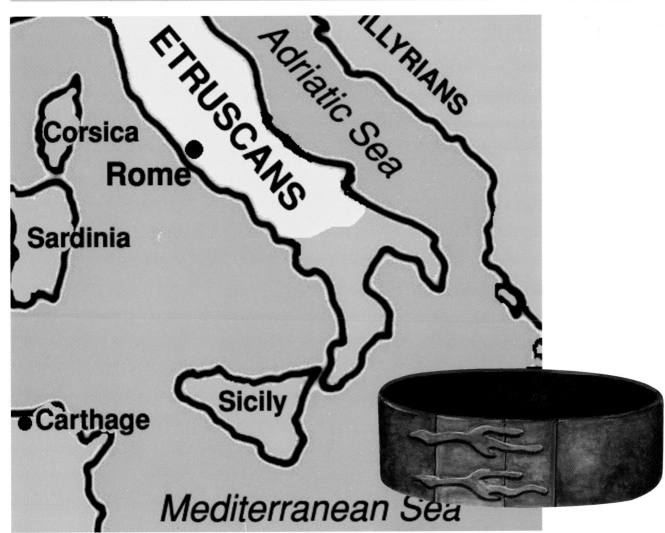

Etruscans – 700 BC to 200 BC

The Etruscans, probably from Asia Minor, settled in central Italy. They used many of the Greek forms of armor, but gave them characteristic Etruscan features such as embossed decoration. Some helmets have extravagant bronze crests, although it is uncertain whether they were for ceremonial purposes, rather than combat. Their body armor was different from the Greeks' so-called scale armor, as it was made up of small plates laced together. Like mail, this form of armor was probably better against slashing blows rather than thrusts.

A Graeco-Etruscan bronze belt (Greek "gordis") and stomach defense (Greek "mitre").

A representation of a coat of paper armor based upon an illustration in the Wu pei chi (AD 1621).

China - from 2000 BC

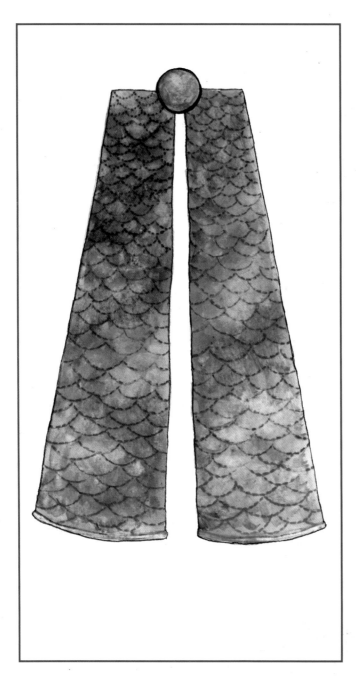

Bronze helmets were made in China during the Shang Dynasty (1520-1030 BC), and a coat-like armor of rhinoceros skin, called kia had been made since the 11th century BC. This was made by sewing together between five and seven layers of rhinoceros skin, around a dummy. Another variant, made from scales, was known as kiai. Helmets continued to be made of this hide until at least about AD 170. The Chinese had also been producing a harder armor by coating leather with a lacquer from an unknown date. Twelve sets of lacquered armor and helmets were discovered in the tomb of the Marquis of Yi, of Zeng, dated to 433 BC. Court armorers existed in the 3rd century BC, and at the Court of the Zhou dynasty a special office of armorers was instituted, the "han jen" ("men who envelop the body with a protective contrivance").

The first emperor of China, Shi Huangdi (259-210 BC), was buried in a huge mausoleum at Lintong, east of Xi'an. One of the terracotta armies discovered in 1974 contained over 1,225 warriors (out of some 8,000 which guard the tomb). Each life-size figure seems to represent an individual, and is shown wearing armor. Men from each section of the army, infantry, archers, and charioteers (and their commanders), wear forms of scale armor, covering the torso and sometimes the shoulders, made from rectangular or square plates, riveted or laced together. This form of lamellar armor was used throughout the East for many centuries, and has been found in tombs in China from about 1400 BC. Mail armor is also shown, and some figures appear to wear shin-guards.

Later China also produced armor made from between 10 and 15 layers of mulberry paper. In the 9th century AD a general raised a 1,000-strong army who wore such paper armor, which apparently was strong enough to stop an arrow. In AD 1040, 30,000 armors of paper were constructed for use by the Shaanxi province garrison. An illustration from the *Wu pei chi*, of AD 1621, shows a form of paper armor.

Reconstruction of a kneeling crossbow-man of the Emperor Shih Huang-ti's army, of about 210 BC. He wears a combination of plate and lamellar armor. It is based on one of the terracotta army figures found at Lintong in 1974. The coloration is based on surviving traces of paint.

Rome – 735 BC to AD 456

The Roman Coolus, or "jockey cap," helmet. It was worn by the Roman army between about 50 BC and AD 50. Like all Roman helmets it would originally have been lined.

According to legend Rome was founded in 735 BC. At the core of the Roman war machine, which created the Roman Empire, stood the Roman soldier. The Romans used a great variety of forms of armor (lorica), and many different materials, such as leather, bronze, and iron.

Armor of mail, in the form of a sleeveless coat, the lorica hamata was used from the 1st century BC and throughout the Roman era, into the 4th century AD.

Scale armor (lorica squamata), made from small plates of bronze or iron, mounted on a fabric or leather backing garment, was cheaper than either mail or plate armor as it required less skill to construct. It was made in an imbricated pattern, giving the appearance of fish scales. It had been in use since the 17th century BC. It may have come to Rome from Greece, where Greeks sometimes reinforced their linen cuirasses with scale armor. Lamellar armor was also used.

Reconstruction of a Roman legionary wearing mail body armor ("lorica hamata"). He wears a Coolus type helmet and an oval shield with squared top and bottom.

Roman imperial Gallic helmet made from iron (mid-1st century BC).

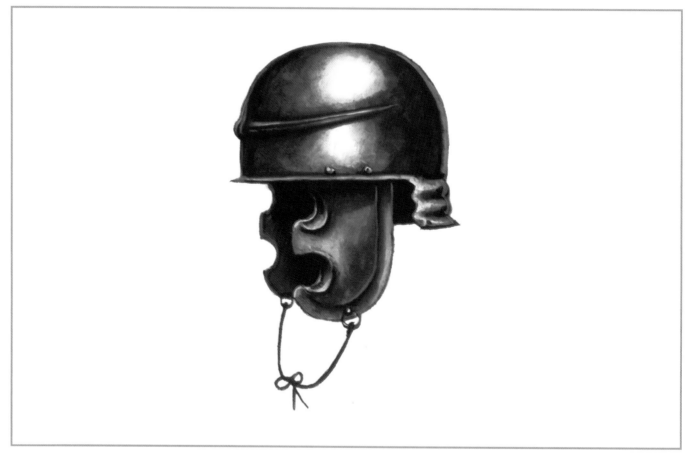

The lorica segmentata, as it is now known, was used between AD 100 to 200 AD. It was built up from about 24 large separate bronze or iron plates, joined together by internal leather straps and some external lacing. Because of this it was flexible. The horizontal plates of the body armor were hinged on one side and buckled on the other. Romans also made great use of the muscled cuirass modeled on the torso, as had the Greeks, and used it until the 5th century AD. Originally it was used only by wealthy soldiers. It may also have been made from hardened leather, but this is not certain. Plate armor for the limbs is known to have been used as well, especially by cavalry men such as Parthian Clibanarius, who used them in the 2nd-3rd centuries AD. Greaves were worn by centurions to protect the shins. Different types of helmet developed including the bronze Coolus, or "jockey cap", form (about 50 BC - AD 50). Made from one piece, it had a broad rear plate fanning out to protect the neck and also large hinged cheek-pieces to protect the sides of the face. It may have originated from the Coolus area of Marne, in Gaul (France). The imperial Gallic helmet of iron, with deeper and broader neck-guard, became the later (AD 50-150) norm. They are probably the most widely known helmets, but even within these two types there were enormous stylistic variations.

The shields of the legionnaires were originally oval, and then evolved into the large rectangular shields (scutum), with central boss by the second half of the 1st century AD. They curved around the body to give more protection.

The one-piece Roman helmet was abandoned in the 3rd century AD, when the skull began to be made from two or more pieces. These so-called "ridge" helmets are precursors of the 4th-century spangenhelm.

Reconstruction of a Roman legionary, wearing laminated body armor and an imperial Gallic helmet of the second half of the 1st century AD. He carries a short stabbing sword ("gladius") on his right side together with a spear ("pilum") and shield ("scutum").

These forms of helmet were worn by gladiators known as "Myrmillo" who were armed with sword and shield, and sometimes fought the "Retiarius."

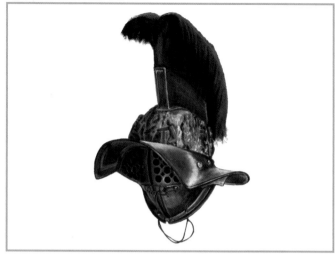

Armors of the Gladiators

Gladiators wore various forms of armor, some particularly designed for the sport, although it is not exactly clear which type of gladiator wore which type of armor. The first gladiators used a large quantity of Samnite armor, captured in 308 BC. These gladiators became known as Samnites. The Samnites fought with a sword (gladius), lance (hasta), and a shield (scutum). They wore a leather or metal greave (ocrea) on the left leg, and a sleeve on the right arm. Their visored helmet (galea) bore a crest and plume. As a group they were succeeded by the Hoplomachi.

Thracians wore bands of leather (fasciae) around their legs, as well as two greaves. They carried a curved sword (sical) and a square or round buckler (parno). Gauls wore fish designs on their helmets, and fought with sword and shield. The Gauls were superseded by the Myrmillo, named after a sea-fish.

The best known gladiator is probably the Retiarius, who was equipped as a fisherman. He fought with the net and fascina (trident). He had no helmet, but wore leg-bands and on the left shoulder a leather or metal defense (galerus). One surviving *galerus*, from Pompeii, is decorated with a crab, dolphin, and anchor. The opponent of the Retiarius was usually the Myrmillo.

The Myrmillo, from the second half of the 1st century AD, used the manica (a laminated arm defense) worn on the right (sword) arm, which also protected part of the hand. They fought with sword and shield, and wore a large helmet with a wide brim, high crest, and an opening visor, which enclosed the entire face. The helmet could also bear a representation of a fish.

There were also gladiators who fought each other on horseback, the Andabatae. They were clad in mail, and wore a sightless vizored helmet, and have been described as looking like *"machines lowered into the arena to be abandoned there."* To win they had to strike at the "joints of the cuirass." The Eques, also wearing a mail cuirass, fought with round shield and lance. Cavalry sport armor included helmets that covered the full face and greaves.

Court gladiators, unlike most gladiators who were slaves, prisoners of war, or condemned criminals, were freemen who fought in splendid armor of embossed gold. Julius Caesar (about 100-44 BC) provided armor of silver, and Nero (AD 37-68), reputedly, of carved amber. The sale of the belongings of the assassinated Emperor Commodus (AD 161-192) included bejeweled pieces, set with precious stones.

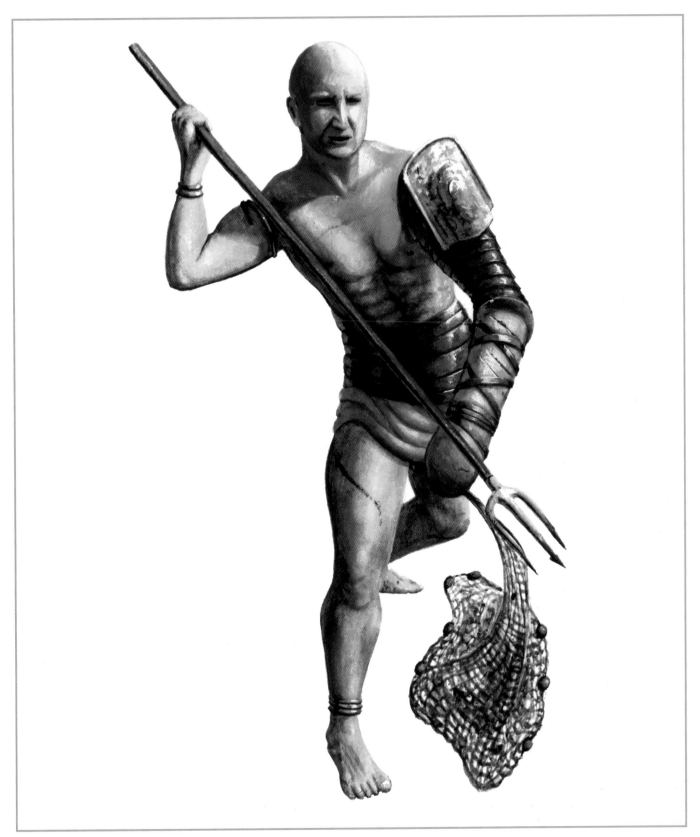

Probably the best-known gladiator was the "Retiarius." He wore little armor apart from a shoulder defense on his left arm, and fought with trident, net, and dagger.

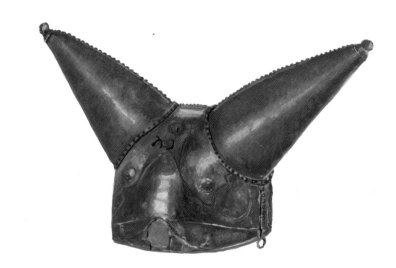

A Celtic horned helmet made of bronze, of about 100 BC, probably for ceremonial use. It was discovered in the River Thames, in London.

Celtic Europe - 100 BC

As the Roman Empire expanded, they fought against many tribes, including the Celts. The Celts were skilled metal-workers in both bronze and iron. They fought with long rectangular shields and conical helmets. Horned helmets survive from the 1st century BC, but they are probably for ceremonial or parade use only. Beautiful examples of Celtic armor survive, such as the Battersea shield of about 200-100 BC. The bronze plates of this shield originally covered a wooden interior, and are set with studs of red glass.

Europe - AD 500 to 1066

After the fall of the Roman Empire in AD 456 European peoples continued to use and develop armor, often based on Roman forms. Mail continued to be used, but armor made of large metal plates went out of fashion. Examples of stunning craftsmanship survive from these so-called 'Dark Ages.' At Vendel in Sweden grave finds dating from around AD 600 include a lavishly decorated helmet. The top of the iron skull of the helmet has a reinforcing comb and decorative eyebrow reinforcements. The face is protected by a "spectacle" vizor, with pierced eye-holes, from which a mail hanging would have been suspended.

The body was protected by mail armor, along with small long splints of iron over the lower abdomen and the lower arms. What may be splints for shins, dating from about AD 650-750, have been found at Valsgarde in Sweden.

The Saxons, originally a Germanic and Danish people, settled in England during the Roman occupation. Later, after the Romans had departed, the Saxons formed kingdoms, which were often at war with each other.

Armor from about AD 625 has been found at Sutton Hoo, in Suffolk, England, including a helmet that has face, cheek, and neck-guard made of iron plates. It has stylistic similarities to one of the helmets found at Vendel in Sweden, but it also resembles Roman cavalry and parade helmets and the ridge helmets of the 4th and 5th centuries. The whole helmet was covered with decorated tinned-bronze foil plates, and the raised eyebrows and mustache were inlaid with silver and garnets. It probably belonged to a royal burial, perhaps that of

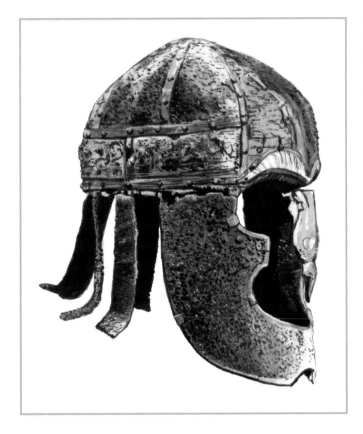

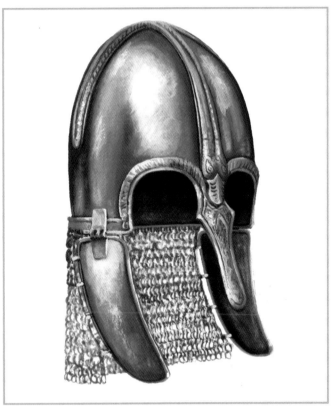

Left: The Anglian helmet, of about AD 750. It was discovered in 1982 at Coppergate, York, England. It is richly decorated with animal ornament and bears a Latin inscription, which includes the name "Oshere," perhaps the name of the original owner of the helmet.

Far left: Helmet from Vendel, Uppland, Sweden. It is made from iron, and the skull is covered by sheets of bronze which portray bands of warriors. About AD 530-600.

Raedwald, king of East Anglia. Although it shows just how richly helmets and armor worn by the wealthy could be decorated, not all armor was so highly decorated.

These forms of helmet are generally classified as spangenhelm. Spangenhelm are round, conical helmets made up of an iron or bronze band (spangen) with arches. The spaces in between the arches are filled with four or more riveted plates, of leather, horn, or metal. The spangenhelm often included an integral or separate nasal bar to protect the face. Some have crests in the shape of boars, as described in *Beowulf*, and as found on one example from Benty Grange. The Benty Grange helmet has spaces filled with horn, and the bronze boar was probably fitted with boar hairs to give a more impressive appearance.

Another helmet found at Coppergate, York, dates to about AD 755. This helmet is made up of a number of segments riveted together with four decorated reinforcing bands running cross-ways over the skull. Cheek-pieces and a long nose-guard protect the face. The neck is protected by a mail neck-guard, made up of over 2,000 individual links. The helmet is inscribed with the name Oshere, presumably that of the maker or owner, and a Christian inscription, possibly an invocation for protection in battle.

Leather jerkins appear to have been the predominant Saxon body armor, although the rich also wore armor of mail, and small strips of metal were sometimes used on the torso and limbs. A mail hood, healsborg, may have also been worn by the rich. Remnants of a mail shirt made of riveted and butted links, the hauberk (a corruption of *healsborg*), were also found at Sutton Hoo, again fitting descriptions found in *Beowulf*, where it is called a byrnie, of fine "meshed" mail:

"His Byrnie shone, a cunning net sewn, with the smith's skill." (*Beowulf*, l.405.)

Most mail shirts were waist-length, with dagged lower edges, but some were longer, reaching to the knee.

The remains of a wooden shield were also found at Sutton Hoo. It was circular, covered in leather, and had an iron boss riveted to the center. It was decorated with gilt metal fittings and a gilt bronze rim. Such circular shields were constructed by butting and gluing together between 3-9 planks of solid wood (such as linden). The front was covered with ox hide. A hole was made in the center of the planks, and the boss fastened over this. The shield was held by a grip riveted across the central hole behind the boss. The shields may also have had neck straps.

Despite Victorian paintings and Hollywood images, which show the Vikings and Danes wearing horned or winged helmets, such helmets were never worn in battle. The helmets most often worn were of conical and spangenhelm form. Some had nasal bars, others were of the "spectacle" face-guard type, as found at Vendel and at the 10th-century grave at Gjermundbu. The conical helmet is perhaps best represented by the St. Wenceslas helmet, of about 935. Some helmets seem to have had painted designs, or "herkumbul" (war-marks), for identification purposes, and others were named. King Adils, a 10th-century Welsh warlord, wore a helmet called "Hildigolt" (War-Boar), which may be a reference to a crest in the form of a boar.

The mail shirt, the brynja or hringskyrta, was usually of waist length (though some may have been knee- or calf- length, such as that of Harald Hardrada (1015-66), King of Norway from 1045, which was named "Emma"), with elbow length sleeves. Some brynja were given names like "Blue-shirt," "The Gray Clothes of Odin," and "War-net." Mail shirts were comparatively effective, but they could be overcome:

"(Thorolf) thrust his spear through the breast of Hring, through the coat of mail and his body, so that it came out between his shoulders; he raised him on the spear over his head, and struck the shaft down into the ground. The jarl expired on the spear."
(Egil's Saga, Ch. 51-6)

Other forms of body armor included leather armor padded with moss or wool and reindeer-hide armor. Metal splints could also have been worn on the arms and lower legs. Armor known as spanga-byrnja may have referred to byrnies with metal plates.

The Vikings carried a round wooden shield with a central boss, which could be strengthened with iron bands. It might be covered in leather, and have a metal rim. The center of the interior of the shield was hollowed out to accommodate the hand-grip, and the raised dome of the boss protected the hand. Shields were given names such as "The War Linden," "Battle-Shelterer," and "The Sun of Battle." Some shields were also decorated:

"Sigurd rode away. His shield was...covered with red gold, and on it was painted a dragon, and in the same way were colored his helmet, saddle, and armour'"
(Volsunga Saga, Ch. 22)

Though the shields were effective, the warrior's legs were prone to attack:

"Egil ran forward and at once struck him, he went so close that Ljolt stepped back, and his shield did not cover him. Then Egil smote him above the knee and cut off his leg. Ljolt fell, and at once died."
(Egil's Saga, Ch. 17)

The shields could be slung along the side of the Viking long ships for protection at sea (a practice apparently continued by their descendants, the Normans, according to the Bayeux Tapestry, which shows Norman ships with rows of "kite" shields).

The Vikings settled over a vast area, from across the Atlantic in the West, to Russia in the East. The west of Scotland remained under their control until the Battle of Largs (AD 1263).

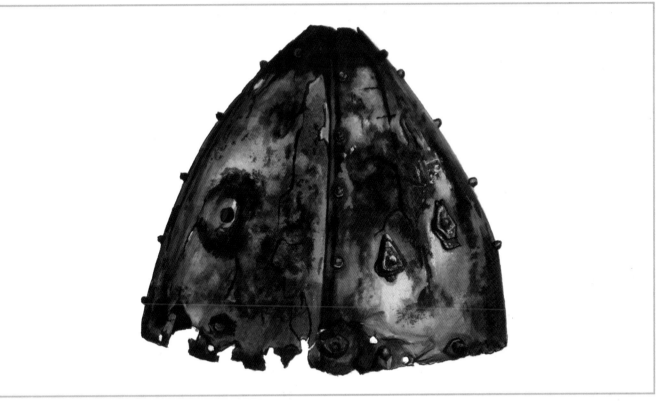

Conical helmet of spangenhelm form, 10th to 11th century, Polish or Russian.
It is made up of four iron plates held together by nails, and lacks its nose-guard.

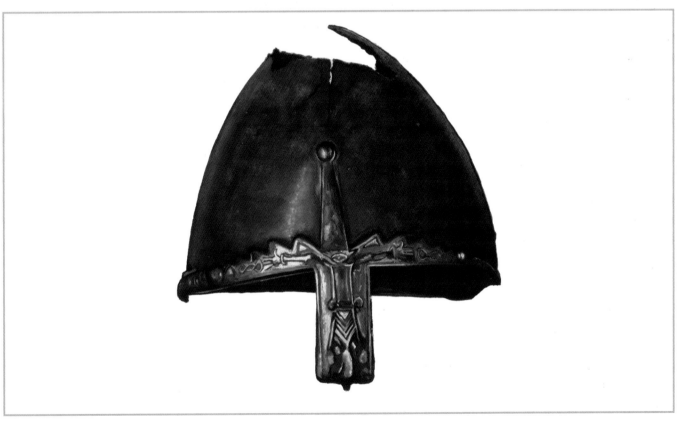

The 'helmet of Saint Wenceslas,' which is preserved in Prague Cathedral. Dating to the 9th-10th century, it is of conical form and one-piece construction. To protect the face, it has an applied nasal bar.

A mail hauberk made from interlocking metal rings, which created a flexible form of armor. Usually the end of each ring was riveted together.

Normans - 1066 to 1099

When the Normans invaded England in 1066, their opponents, the Saxons, wore armor that had altered little in the previous 200 years. The main source of information regarding the armor of this period is the Bayeux Tapestry. This tapestry shows the full story of the Norman invasion of England, which culminated in the Battle of Hastings. It is probably English and is in fact an embroidery rather than a woven cloth. It was made between 1066 and 1082. Most of the hard armor shown in the tapestry is of mail rather than plate. The coat of mail, the hauberk, was worn at calf length, and was split up the front and back to groin level to facilitate horse riding. It could weigh about 32lbs (14 kg). Some hauberks are shown with a square or rectangular area on the chest. It is not at all clear what this actually was, it may have been a mail reinforcement. The hauberk was worn over a garment of some kind, one that may well have been padded. Owing to damage to the Bayeux Tapestry and some inaccurate restorations, it was thought for some time that the mail hauberk was worn directly on the skin. This would have been unbearably uncomfortable. Sleeves of mail extended to the elbow and mail leggings, known as chausses, might also be worn. Longer sleeves of mail, extending to the wrist, may well have been the prerogative of wealthier nobles. For the whole period 900-1200 one mail hauberk is known to survive.

Conical helmets were worn, some made from one piece of iron, others from a number of pieces, in the manner of the earlier spangenhelm. The nasal bars were sometimes so wide that they obscured the wearer's features and made recognition difficult. It is recorded that William the Conqueror (about 1028-1087) had to raise his helmet in the midst of the Battle of Hastings to show his soldiers that he was still alive. Some helmets may have been painted to identify the wearer.

As new equipment and techniques were introduced, the mailed heavy cavalry became the core of the army. The widespread introduction of the stirrup and the high-cantled saddle (pommel to the fore, arcon to the rear) provided a secure mobile fighting platform for the Norman knight. Standing in the stirrups, firmly held in the saddle, he could now deliver stronger blows with his sword, and, more importantly, couch the 12-foot (3.5-meter) lance of ash firmly under his arm, and charge an enemy. Before this the lance was used to stab, prod, lunge, and throw at the enemy. The weight and speed of horse and rider were now combined at the moment of impact. An account of Hastings describes its effect: *"a French soldier…raised his shield and struck…with his lance on the breast, so that the iron passed out of his back."* By now the knight's horse itself was a weapon in its own right. The war-horse, a

stallion, had been bred and trained to bite, flail with its hooves, and trample enemies.

The Normans are shown using large shields covering the unprotected left side of the user's body from shoulder to ankle. With their rounded top edges and two long edges coming together in a point, these shields have been given the modern name kite shield. This shield could be held by the hand using a grip, or a series of straps, known as the enarme, or it could hung around the neck by another longer strap called the guige. Both grips could be used together.

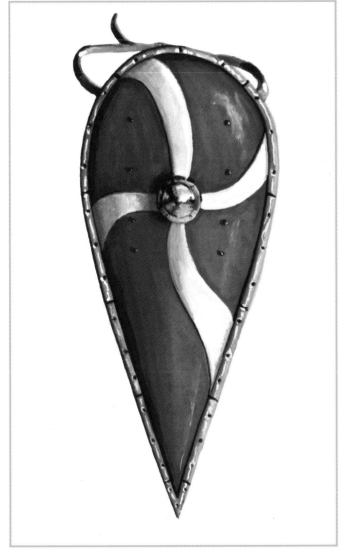

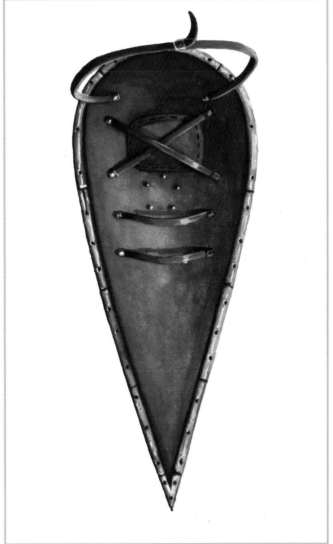

Front and rear view of a Norman kite shield. It was made of wood and covered in leather. Sometimes it bore painted decoration. A rim of metal protected the edges and the two types of grips allowed the shield to be borne either on the arm or slung around the neck.

The "kettle-hat" or "chapel-de-fer" was a simple iron helmet with a brim. It was a form, which would remain popular for many centuries as it offered good protection, ventilation, and vision.

Europe - 1100 to 1199

The main body armor of the 12th century continued to be the mail hauberk, which was now worn over a quilted garment called a gambeson or aketon. Mail extensions of the sleeves developed, called mufflers, which covered the outer parts of the hands. These hung loose at the wrist until required for battle, and were then slipped on. The palm area was left open, or covered in thin leather so as to allow the warrior to be able to grasp the weapon more firmly and comfortably.

New forms of helmet appeared, including the flat-topped helm, which had a fixed vizor covering the entire face. This led to problems of identification, and to alleviate these a formal system of recognized designs, known as heraldry, started to develop, particularly in German lands. Crests were worn on the tops of helmets, and badges, called blazons, on shields. Surcoats, or coat-armors, were worn over the mail hauberks for the first time, although to start with they were plain and white. A 14th-century poem describes them as protecting the armor from rain and keeping it clean. As the garment was loose-fitting, this seems extremely doubtful. In fact these surcoats were probably copied from the Saracen enemies of the Crusader knights, who wore white loose-flowing garments to help reflect some of the heat of the sun. Heraldic devices were soon painted on the European surcoats.

The spangenhelm remained in use but was falling out of favor. The nasal became smaller, and was often absent, as it could prove to be a liability. Helmets like this were often carried by the nasal, as depicted in the Bayeux Tapestry, and it is possible that William de Cahaignes captured King Stephen (about 1097-1154), at the Battle of Lincoln (1141), by catching hold of his helmet's nasal bar and crying *"Here, everyone, I have the King!"*

Other forms of helmet included the kettle-hat, or chapel-de-fer, which remains in use to this day, in a very modified form, as the service helmet of many armies. It has a round bowl-shaped skull, with a wide, down turned brim running all the way around its edge.

Helmets were laced under the chin. This stopped

Helmets worn in the 12th century included not only the conical one-piece construction form, but also flat-topped helmets with nasals.

them from falling off or sliding round and temporarily blinding the wearer. At the Battle of Tagliacozzo (1268) an incident of such blinding is recorded. The helmet of Guy de Montfort slipped over his eyes, and he lashed out wildly, wounding his friend Alard de St. Valery who was rushing to his rescue. A mail head-piece developed, which could be worn with helmets. This was the coif-de-maille. It had a flap of mail at the cheek, the ventail, which, like the mufflers, hung loose from the cheek until battle approached, when it was drawn up and laced near the ear on the other side of the face. This protected the mouth and chin area.

Mail armor, worn over the gambeson, although quite effective against slashing blows, could not halt the penetrative power of an arrow or lance. Mail could also be driven into wounds, and could not prevent bones from being broken by heavy blows. Dirty and rusting broken links and compound fractures could result in wounds turning septic and fatal. Moreover, despite lacings at key points, such as wrists and knees, mail still hung heavily and mostly from the shoulders. To counter these problems, an ancient form of body armor was reinvented, that of plate.

The earliest known surviving reference to medieval plate armor occurs in about 1190, when metal plates were used on the chest. These plates may also have been made of cuir-bouilli, leather that was heated in molten wax or oil, and then moulded into the desired shape.

Increasingly the face became protected by plate, which together with the neck-guard, developed into a defense that entirely enclosed the head. This was known as the helm, and had slits to allow vision and breathing.

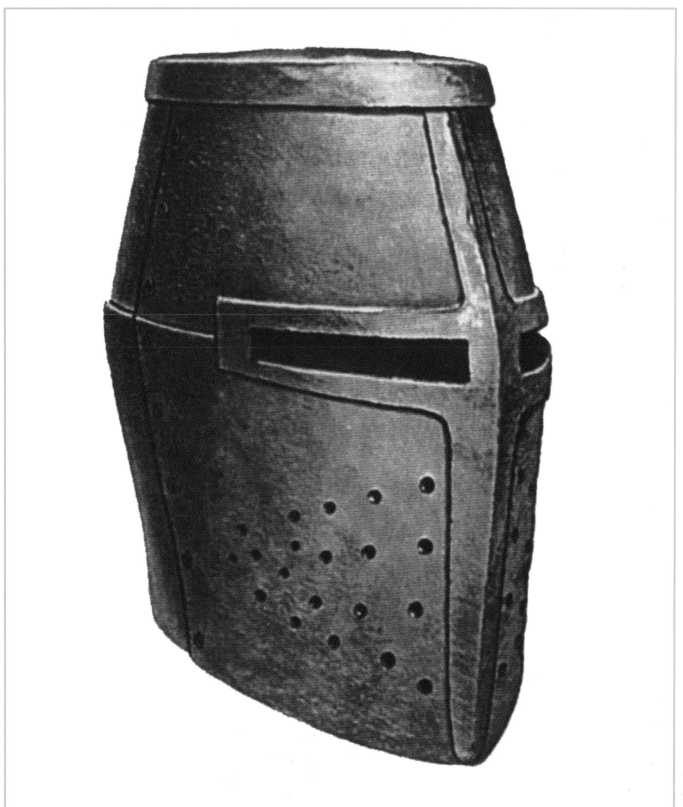

This helm of more solid construction has better protection for the whole face.

Europe - 1200 to 1299

By about 1250 many different types of helmet were in use at the same time, including large cylindrical helms, flattened spangenhelms, and kettle-hats. Plate armor was becoming more widespread, and lower leg defences, called greaves, made of metal and/or leather, were worn. They were tied at the back of the leg. Padded cuisses were worn on the thighs. Poleyns, which protected the knees, were attached to the cuisses. Elbow protectors, couters, seem to have appeared slightly later, in about 1260. The first parts to become plate-armored were the extremities that were most vulnerable, particularly for those who rode on horseback, but another important factor in the redevelopment of plate armor was technological. Armorers at this time do not appear to have been capable or confident enough to make larger metal plates. Instead, the limbs were protected with small plates.

At the Battle of Mansurah (1250), during the 7th Crusade (1248-54), Hugues de Ecot and Raoul de Wanou received three lance wounds in the face, and Frederic de Loupey was lanced in the back so *that his blood gushed from his body as if from the bung hole of a barrel.* Evard de Siverey had his nose sliced off, and it was left dangling over his lips. From this evidence it is clear that mail hauberks could not stop the penetrative power of a lance strike. The wounds to the face imply that open-faced helmets, such as the kettle-hats, were being worn. Given that this battle was fought in the hot climate of what is now the Middle East, this is perhaps understandable.

Jean de Joinville (about 1224-1311), a contemporary chronicler, tells us with relief that he himself was injured in only five places by arrows, although his horse was hit 15 times. It was probably the combination of mail and the padded gambeson that saved him from more serious wounds.

His horse was obviously not so lucky. Armor for horses developed later. The Vikings and Saxons usually dismounted before engaging in combat. From the mid-13th century illustrations survive showing some horses covered in a bard, or trapper, of mail. Richard I, known as Coeur de Lion or Lionheart (1157-99), first came across examples of this when 140 of the 200 horses captured at the Battle of Gisors (1190) were *clad in iron.* A decorative cloth covering the bard, or just the horse, and known as the housing or couverture, had been in use since about 1180. One housing covered the head and withers of the horse, the other the crupper, behind the saddle. It went to hock length, and was split at the front and back to allow the animal freedom to move. From the surviving evidence it is difficult to tell whether or not the housing was padded, and whether mail was worn beneath it.

During the 12th century the Norman kite shield became smaller, but it was only in the 13th century that the shield took the shorter heater shape (another modern term, used because the shape is similar to that of a flat iron). These smaller shields were much less cumbersome and easier to wield.

At the close of the 13th century metal gauntlets for the hands appear, and start to replace "the mailed fist."

Reconstruction of a knight of about 1250. The knight is shown with his laced-up mail ventail around his face, and his helm. His hands are enclosed by mail mufflers, and on his lower legs he wears a pair of mail chausses. This is based on an illustration by Matthew Paris.

An Italian vizored basinet of about 1390. The pointed vizor is detachable, being held in place by pins inserted in hinges on either side of the helmet. It has a mail aventail to protect the neck.

Europe - 1300 to 1399

Armor of the early 14th century was not that much different from that of the late 13th century. However, as the century wore on armor construction changed radically, from being mainly mail to mainly plate. 1377 saw the start of what would become "The Hundred Years' War" (which actually ended in 1453), and this no doubt contributed to the need and desire for technological change. Armor evolved to counter the widespread use of more powerful missile weapons, such as the longbow and crossbow, and percussive weapons like the sword and mace.

Knights continued to wear the padded and quilted garment, the aketon or gambeson, beneath their mail hauberk. Sometimes the garment was worn without the hauberk as an independent defense. By the 1320s a coat of plates was common. It was made from iron plates riveted to, or between, layers of material. This may have developed from strengthened surcoats of the latter part of the 13th century, when small iron plates were attached by rivets to the surcoat.

The front of the lower legs was now protected by shin-guards known as demi-greaves, or schynbalds. By about 1320 sabatons, armor for the feet, were in use. Armor for the arms, called vambraces, rapidly followed. The upper arm was covered by a plate called the upper cannon and the lower arm by the lower cannon. Usually of "gutter" shape, the plates were worn over the sleeves of the mail hauberk. As early as the 1330s the lower arm was completely enclosed by two hinged plates. By the mid 1330s tube-like upper and lower cannons were joined by couters at the elbow. Like the armor for the leg, these were strapped and buckled on.

By the close of the 13th century heraldry was a fully developed "art," with its own codes and practices. Heraldic arms were also seen on ailettes, small squares of fabric or soft material, worn on top of the shoulders. A description in 1313 tells of one

Reconstruction of Edward the Black Prince in combat in the latter part of his life. He is depicted fighting without his great helm, which could be worn over the basinet.

It is based upon his copper gilt effigy at Canterbury Cathedral, England. He fought at battles such as Crécy (1346) and Poitiers (1356). His armor is mostly of plate. He wears a jupon over the armor, which bears the royal arms. He was called the Black Prince because he reputedly wore "blackened" armor, although there is no evidence for this.

ARMOR FOR HORSES AND OTHER ANIMALS

Horse armor was probably first developed in Central Asia. The ancient Greeks used chaffrons, and by the Battle of Cunaxa (AD 401), chaffrons, crinets, and cruppers, made of iron scales, were in use. Armor for horse and rider developed together. In the late 13th century plates of leather and metal were used to protect the horse the chaffron protected the horse's head, and the peytral its chest. By 1325 plates had been introduced to protect other parts of the horse, such as the flanchards on the flanks and the crupper on the rear. Necks were originally protected by long mail collars, which were eventually superseded by a series of laminated plates known as the crinet. Around 1480 Maximilian I seems to have ordered a horse armor from Lorenz Helmschmid of Augsburg, which covered "all parts" of the horse from head to fetlock, including articulated joints for the legs. A painting survives showing such a horse armor but no horse armor has been found identical to the one in the painting, only portions of similar ones.

In India elephants have been used for war since at least the 3rd century BC and up until the 19th century AD. Indian war elephants were used by the Macedonians in the campaigns of Alexander the Great (356- 323 BC). With howdahs on their backs, from which archers and spearmen could fight, they made excellent mobile fighting platforms and command posts. One such early 17th-century armor, made of small plates and mail, survives at the Royal Armouries, Leeds, originally in the collection of Robert Clive of India (1725-74), who acquired it at the Battle of Plassey in 1757. The tusks of elephants could also be armed with steel 'swords.'

Dogs wore armor in Italy, Spain, Germany, and the Low Countries. A German inventory of 1542 lists two "white" (steel) armors for dogs. A 17th-century Hundepanzer ("dog-armor") survives, made from four layers of linen, covered with buttonhole-stitched eyelets.

Hundepanzer (dog-armor) from Wartburg, Germany, 17th century. This "eyelet" coat was made from four layers of linen and was probably worn by a boarhound.

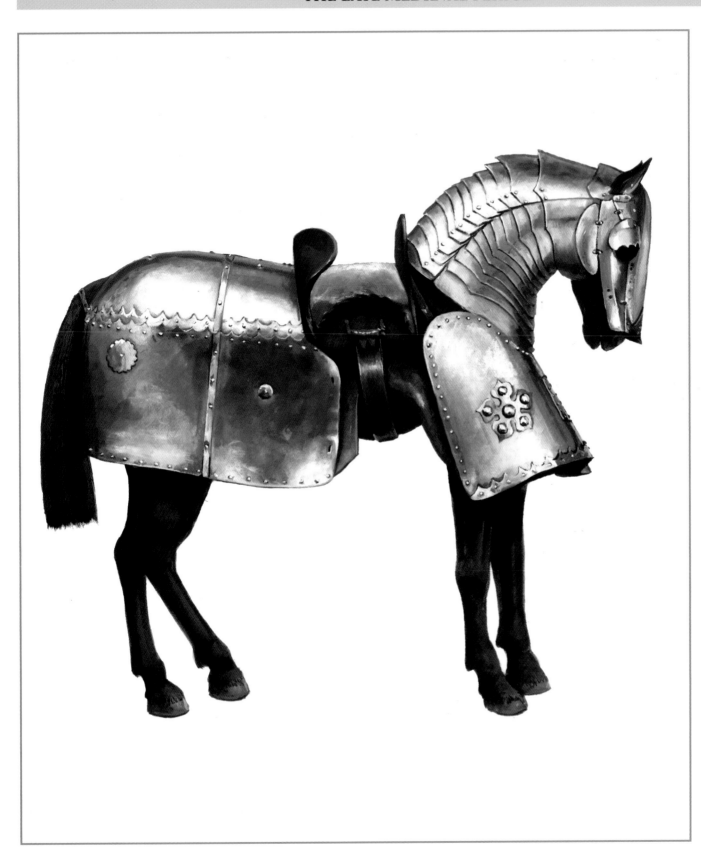

Armor for a horse, made in Milan, Italy, about 1450-60, by Pier Innocenza da Faerno. It is the earliest surviving complete armor of this type, and consists of large solid plates. The head is protected by the chaffron, and the neck by a laminated crinet. The peytral protects the chest and the crupper the rear half of the horse.

pair of ailettes made of parchment and pearls. Sometimes whalebone or metal was used, but it is generally felt that these accoutrements were for heraldic display, rather than protection. Although their exact method of attachment is not known, they must have been laced on in some way. They appear to have been worn until the 1340s.

Helmet design changed considerably. The basinet generally retained its conical form, but became more pointed. This increased its effectiveness in warding off sword blows. The basinet covered the back of the neck as well as the sides of the face, giving even more protection. From around the1320s-30s, a mail aventail was attached to the lower edges of the helmet. This mail tippet was secured to a leather band, which had holes in it. The leather band was fitted over staples, vervelles, which ran along the side and back edges of the helmet. The aventail protected not only the neck and throat but also upper shoulders.

Helmets with movable face-guards, vizors, may have appeared at the close of the 13th century, but it was in the 14th century that their use became widespread. Both basinets and great helms sometimes had vizors. The great helm was worn in combat, over the basinet, providing yet another level of protection for the head. It is often shown in contemporary illustrations, such as the Lutterell Psalter of about 1340. The basinets had internal padding and probably a form of internal webbing to allow it to be worn without the mail coif.

The vizor took many forms, and had slits, sights, to allow the wearer to see and holes, breaths, for the wearer to breathe. Breaths were often only on the right side of the vizor, as opposing warriors on horseback usually crossed the lance, held in the right hand, over the neck of the horse, so facing each other left to left. The vizor was attached to the skull of the helmet by pivots at either side, which enabled the vizor to be raised when not in use and allow easier breathing. These side pivots later developed into pinned hinges, which made the vizor easier to remove for cleaning, repairing, and replacing. To deflect sword blows the vizors became bulbous or pointed, looking like the snout of an animal. They

were known as houndskull basinets. This type of helmet was preferred in combat situations to the much more stuffy, claustrophobic, and heavier great helm, which was gradually relegated to tournament use. On top of the helm were worn fabulous crests, which could be made from leather, parchment, whalebone, or feathers.

By the 1340s the coat of plates had taken the form of horizontal steel hoops riveted to a leather garment, which was often covered in velvet. It is possible that a few single breastplates were in use at this time, although they would have been rare.

The plate defenses of the limbs became even more extensive and complicated. By the mid-14th century the upper arms were fully enclosed by two plates, which were hinged and strapped together. The couter, the elbow defense, was connected to this upper portion of the arm armor by a series of small plates, or lames. The lower arms were connected to the couters in a similar manner. In effect the armor of the whole arm became one flexible unit. The shoulders were also covered with plate. Sometimes these round or shell-shaped defences were decorated using animal motifs, such as lion heads.

The hands were protected by gauntlets, which had cuffs of bell-shaped plate. The fingers had several individual lames to give greater flexibility.

Armor for the legs also continued to improve. After 1340 cuisses were sometimes of brigandine construction (with small lames connected in an overlapping and flexible manner by rivets). The rivet heads could be gilded as a decorative feature. The hemispherical poleyn, encasing the front and sides of the knee, also appeared about 1340, and it had a side-wing, a fan-like extension, on the outer side to protect the back of the knee. It was attached to the cuisse, as the couter was to the arm defense.

Solid breastplates became common during the 1360s-70s. A skirt made up of laminated horizontal hoops of plate, the fauld, was worn to protect the hips. The backplate and breastplate came together to create a tight figure-hugging "wasp" waist. This was thought to be flattering and very fashionable, and is found on many effigies, such as that of Edward the Black Prince (1330-76) in Canterbury Cathedral.

His body armor is shown covered by a snug-fitting quilted jupon, a development of the earlier surcoat, which bears his heraldic devices.

Greaves completely enclosed the lower legs and they were connected by small lames to the poleyns together with the plates now making up the cuisses, the legs also became a single flexible system of defense.

Gauntlets, as well as breastplates, reflected fashion by developing hour-glass-shaped cuffs, the neck being at the wrist. The knuckles were protected by raised, sometimes pointed areas, called gadlings, which could be used as "knuckle-dusters" if necessary.

The so called 'lance rest' also appears at this time.

This metal bracket, on the upper right side of the breastplate, should perhaps be more correctly called the "lance stop." It was there not so much to "rest" the weight of the lance on it as to help disperse the shock of the lance throughout the breastplate, and to stop it slipping back through the hand when it hit its target. To be effective it obviously needed to be attached to a solid breastplate, not one made up of separate plates. They are commonly found after 1380.

Many contemporary illustrations of The Hundred Year's War show these types of armor in use, as do monumental effigies, such as that of Sir Humphrey Littlebury (died 1350). This effigy and others also show the sword suspended from a fine

ARMORERS' MARKS

When armors are examined closely different stamped marks can often be found. They can be the personal mark of an armorer, or the view mark of the town where the armor was made. If the armor was of the approved standard it gained the mark of the guild, which often alluded to the town of manufacture, such as Augsburg or Nuremberg. Other marks might include arsenal marks.

Seven examples of Italian armorers' marks.

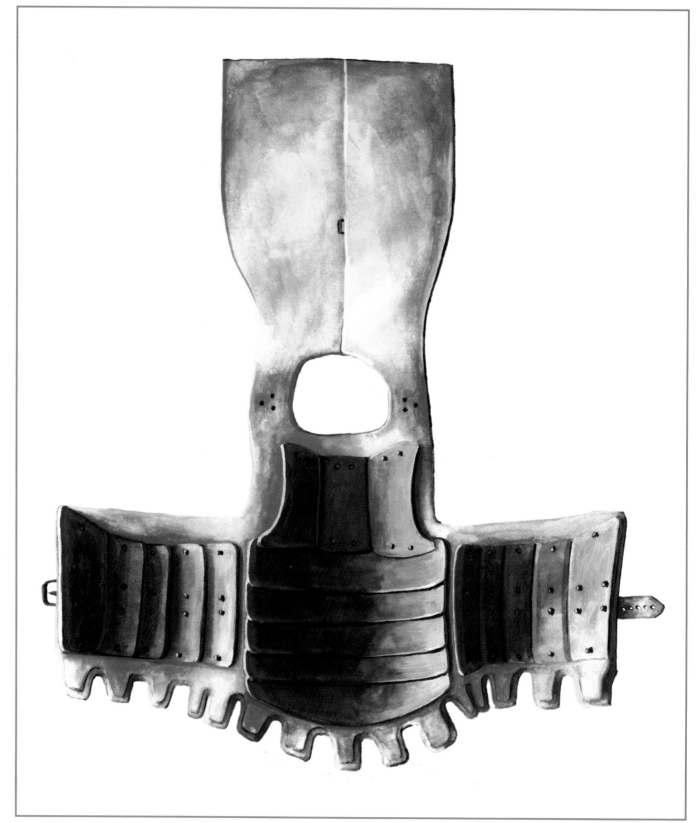

Reconstruction of interior of coat-of-plates, based on the finds from the mass graves from the Battle of Wisby (1361), Gotland, Sweden.
This was fought between the Gotlanders and the Danes.
The coats-of-plates consisted of iron plates riveted to a poncho like foundation garment of leather.

Reconstruction of exterior of coat-of-plates, as worn over a mail hauberk.
The rivet heads on the outside of the garment are clearly visible.

A vizored "black" sallet, made in Germany, about 1490, for a light horseman. Some helmets, such as this example, were covered with painted "heraldic" decoration.

Europe - 1400 to 1499

In the 15th century the European armorers' craft reached its apogee of achievement.

The armors worn in such battles as Agincourt (1415) had evolved from those worn at the end of the 14th century. The body was now totally encased in a steel carapace, literally from head to toe. The breastplate was hinged to the backplate on the left side and was drawn together by straps and buckles on the right. The armholes were protected by small round or rectangular plates known as besagews. Poleyns and couters had now developed deep fan-shaped wings. The mail aventail was still worn, attached to the basinet but was often covered by two or more gorget plates at the throat. Occasionally helms were still worn over the basinets, but more often than not a vizor was worn attached by pinned hinges to the sides of the skull of the helmet.

By the 1420s the basic design of Italian armor had developed. The rounded breastplate narrowed to, and terminated at, the waist. The lower part was protected by a lower breastplate, the plackart. It was attached to the breastplate by straps, which by the mid-15th century had become one central strap. The plackart curved in above the hips and from it was suspended the fauld of three or four plates to protect the lower abdomen. Armor for the back was of similar construction, and all edges, such as neck and armhole, had a rim of rolled steel stop-ribs, to prevent a sword point or arrow-head from glancing over the edge and penetrating the wearer.

The construction of the armor left the areas of the armpit and groin the most vulnerable, because of the need to allow maximum flexibility of the limb joints. Hauberks were still worn beneath the plate armor, sometimes with a small mail skirt attached to the fauld. The groin could further be protected by the addition of a brayette, the equivalent of mail shorts. Arm defenses were still of three elements, and as plate armor was so efficient the shield fell into disuse. To compensate for this Italian armors became "asymmetrical," the rein, or shield, arm having a larger couter than the sword arm. The sword arm was of lighter construction, reflecting the fact that both sword and lance were used on this side. It also had a smaller upper vambrace, cut away to allow the lance to be couched under the arm. The lance-stop was attached securely by a pin, which passed through staples on the breastplate.

It is this type of armor that is depicted frequently in the works of Italian Renaissance artists, such as Piero della Francesca, Uccello, and Mantegna.

The 'Avant' armor made in Milanese workshops about 1440-45. It belonged to a member of the Matsch family of Churburg Castle in the Italian Tyrol. Although the helmet, a barbuta, is slightly later, the rest of the armor is complete, except for the right gauntlet (a modern replacement); the gardbrace for the right shoulder; and the two tassets. It bears the inscription "Avant" six times in punched decoration.

From around 1400 helmet forms diversified further. From 1400 to 1470 the barbuta was a popular type. It is similar to the Ancient Greek Corinthian-type helmet, with a "T"-shaped face opening to allow sight and ventilation. It was a justly popular helmet, allowing much protection and freedom. A similar helmet, the celata, had a broad arched facial opening, the face being mostly uncovered. Sometimes barbutas and celatas were vizored.

Another popular helmet was the armet. It was developed from the basinet. It had a one-piece skull, which terminated at ear level, except at the back, where the steel continued down to the nape of the neck. Hinged cheek-pieces were attached to either side of the skull and were raised to allow the wearer to put it on. The cheek-pieces were then brought down and locked into place by a hook or spring stud over the chin. The face opening was then covered by a detachable pivoted vizor, fixed to the sides of the skull by hinges. A small mail tippet, or aventail, could also be attached around the base of the helmet. Because of its construction the chin defense was comparatively weak and so an extra defense, the buff, or wrapper, was worn. This extra defense was shaped to the lines of the lower half of the helmet, with two laminated gorget plates to protect the throat. It was attached to the armet by a leather strap, which passed around the neck. Another form of the armet helmet, the armet à rondelle, had a steel disc or rondel at the nape of the neck, set on a stem, to protect the wrapper strap from being cut off by an opponent's cut to the back of the neck. The armet remained popular into the 16th century.

German armor evolved differently, though basically using the same pieces. From 1460 the German style is usually known as "Gothic," as it involved finely pointed extremities, and the plates were gracefully curved and fluted. The Victorians invented this term, using it first to describe a style of early medieval architecture with finely pointed and fretted lines. Armor from Germany was also far more symmetrical, especially in the pauldrons (the shoulder defenses), than its Italian counterpart.

At the start of the 15th century the German breastplate was quite box like. However, it became more rounded and was made up of a single plate or a fixed upper and lower plate. Riveted gussets were attached to the armhole to facilitate more movement. The attached breastplate was made up of one piece, which had a deep waist plate. The waist became extremely slender, a very fashionable "wasp-waist."

The whole armor, with its very long pointed, narrow, outlines, was as much a fashion statement as for practical defense. The elegant forms were further exaggerated by the flutings on the plates, and applied gilt brass borders were found on the more expensive armors.

Another very popular form of helmet in Germany and elsewhere was the sallet, which had appeared by the mid-15th century. It probably derived from the celata helmet that was in use in the first decades of the 15th century in Italy. The sallet had a broad open face over which a vizor could be fixed. Alternatively, the helmet could be made from one piece with the sight cut into the leading face. By the mid-15th century it had developed a tail, and from the 1480s this was often laminated. The graceful form of this helmet complemented the shape of the rest of the armor perfectly.

These helmets were often worn together with chin-shaped plates called bevors. Bevors were attached by a strap running around the back of the neck, and had an attachment point on the center of the upper breastplate. Although they provided excellent defense for the lower face they restricted movement and were comparatively uncomfortable to wear (the origin of the word 'bevor' is said to be from the old French "to dribble," which shows what wearing one must have been like). They proved unpopular, and accounts survive of men who were killed because they rushed into battle without their bevor or lowered it temporarily for ventilation. Cornelius, son of the Burgundian Charles the Bold (1433-77), was killed when struck in the face while not wearing a bevor at the Battle of Rupplemonde (1452).

Armor of these types was common throughout conflicts such as the Wars of the Roses in England and the Burgundian Wars in Switzerland.

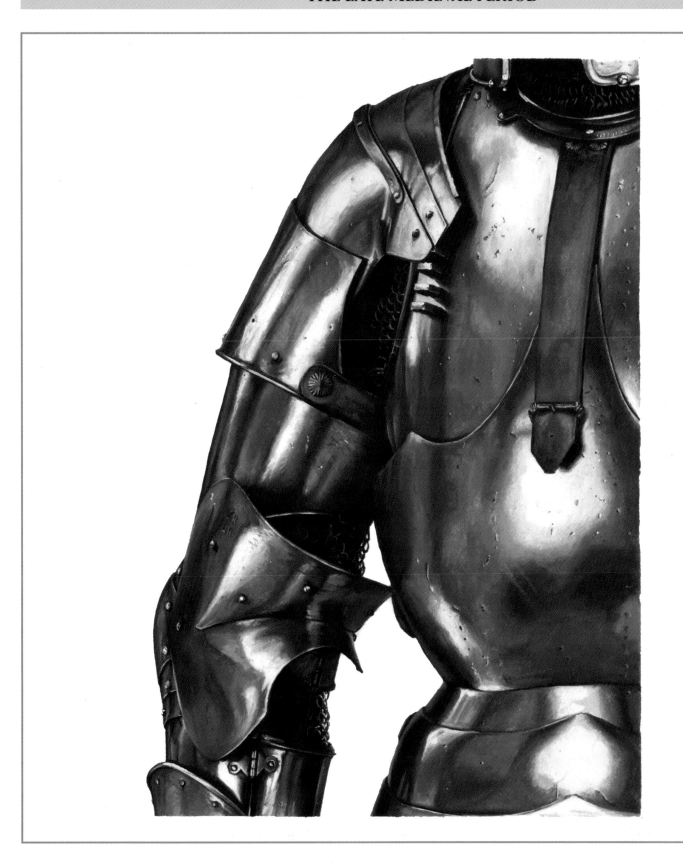

BUCKLES AND STRAPS

Armor was held together by a series of interior straps, called leathers, as this is what they were made of. They were riveted to the individual plates, or lames (hence the term laminated), in such a way as to make the joints flexible. They were of plain buff leather, but external straps, for wrappers, tassets, vambraces, etc., were often covered in velvet, usually red in color. The mounts for these straps could often be of brass, and sometimes were gilded.

NAMING THE PARTS

The "Avant" armor, made in Milan in about 1440-45 provides a key for parts of the armor and their names. Note that the tassets are an additional reconstruction and that the armor lacks a mail skirt beneath the fauld (After Edge & Paddock, 1988).

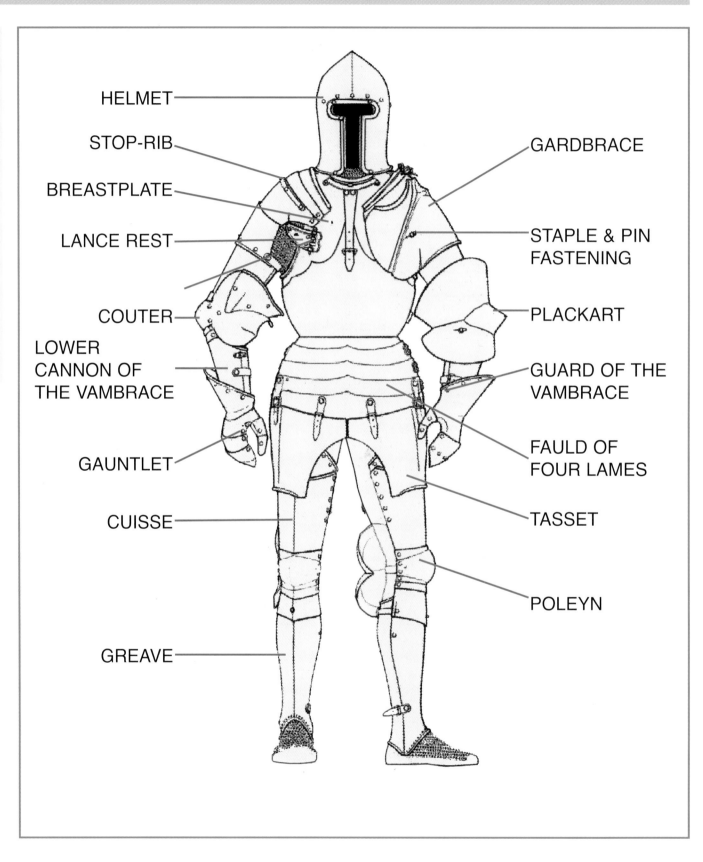

HELMET

STOP-RIB

BREASTPLATE

LANCE REST

COUTER

LOWER CANNON OF THE VAMBRACE

GAUNTLET

CUISSE

GREAVE

GARDBRACE

STAPLE & PIN FASTENING

PLACKART

GUARD OF THE VAMBRACE

FAULD OF FOUR LAMES

TASSET

POLEYN

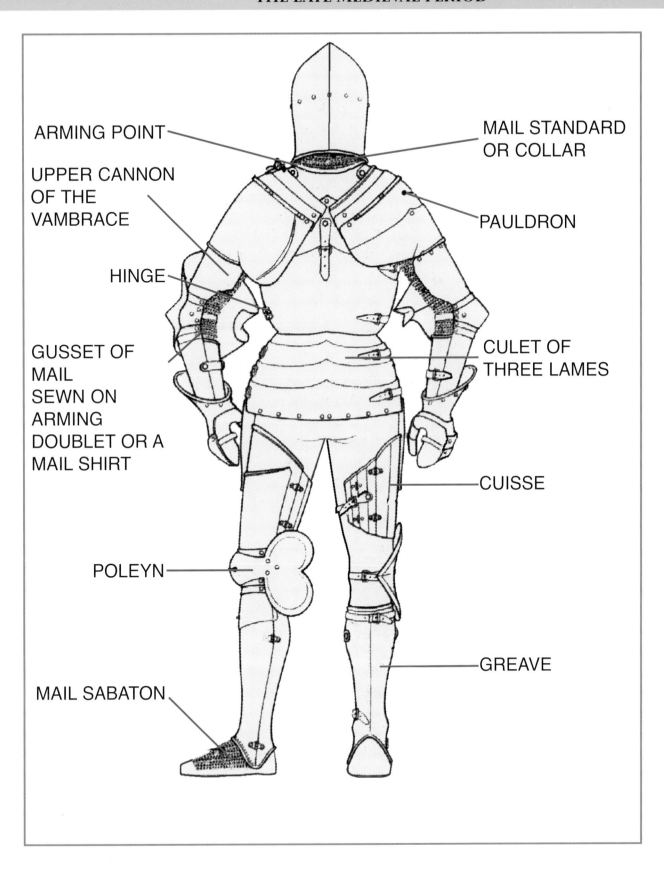

ARMING POINT

UPPER CANNON
OF THE
VAMBRACE

HINGE

GUSSET OF
MAIL
SEWN ON
ARMING
DOUBLET OR A
MAIL SHIRT

POLEYN

MAIL SABATON

MAIL STANDARD
OR COLLAR

PAULDRON

CULET OF
THREE LAMES

CUISSE

GREAVE

In the armor of this century, so effective and pleasing to the eye, Western makers had reached their zenith. Many of the armorers are known by name, and they marked their wares boldly. In Italy the Corio, the Missaglia, and the Negroli families were famous makers. In Germany the Helmschmid family was renowned, as were the Treytz of Innsbruck. The finest armors were not only practical, they were works of art. The extraordinary skills of the armorers are apparent in such features as breastplates, which are thicker at the front than at the sides, and in helmets hammered from one billet of steel. The armor could also be hardened in various ways and in various places for extra protection. All these subtleties were the work of master exponents of the armorer's craft.

In Europe, however, the armor of the knight was about to undergo another radical change, as firepower became even more efficient. Tactics altered, and privilege, wealth, and the associated power began to shift from one group to another.

"HOW A MAN SCHALL BE ARMYD AT HIS ESE…"

Armor had to be put on piece by piece, in a strict order, to fit properly. This usually required the assistance of at least one squire. A contemporary account, The Hastings Manuscript, of the 15th century describes exactly how an armored warrior was prepared for combat.

He schal have noo schirte up on him but a dowbelet of ffustean lynyd with satene cutte full of hoolis, the dowbelet must be strongeli boude there the poyntis muste be sette aboute the greet [bend] of the arme, and the b ste [sic] before and behynde and the gussetis of mayle muste be sowid un to the dowbelet in the bought of the arme, and undir the arme the armynge poyntis must be made of fyne twyne suche as men make stryngis for crossebowes and they muste be trussid small and poyntid as poyntis. Also they muste be wexid with cordeweneris coode, and than they woll neythir recche nor breke. Also a payr' hosyn of stamyn sengill and a peyre of shorte bulwerkis of thynne blanket to put aboute his kneys for chawfynge of his lighernes. Also a payre of shone of thikke cordewene and they must be frette with smal whipcorde thre knottis up on a corde and thre coordis muste be faste sowid un to the hele of the shoo and fyne cordis in the mydill of the soole of the same shoo and that ther be betwene the frettis of the heele and the frettis of the myddil of the shoo the space of three fyngris.

To arme a man. ffirste ye muste sette on Sabatones and tye them up on the shoo with smale poyntis that wol breke. And then griffus [greaves] & then cuisses & the breche of mayle And the tonletis And the brest And the vambras And the rerebras And then glovys. And then hange his daggere upon his right side. And then his shorte swerde upon the lyfte side in a rounde rynge all nakid to pull it oute lightli. And then putte his cote upon his bak And then his basinet pynid up on two greet staplis before the breste with a dowbil bokill behynde up on the bak for to make the basinet sitte juste. And then his long swerde in his hande. And then his pensill in his hande peyntid of seynt George or of oure lady to blesse him with as he gooth towarde the felde and in the felde.

A composite "Gothic" armor for man and horse made in Germany in the late 15th century. The horse armor was probably for Waldemar VI of Anhalt-Zerbst (1450-1508). The head is protected by a sallet and the throat by a bevor.

Armor for the Archduke Sigismund of Tyrol, Augsburg, about 1480. It was made by Lorenz Helmschmid in the fluted "Gothic" style and represents the apogee of the art of the German armorer.

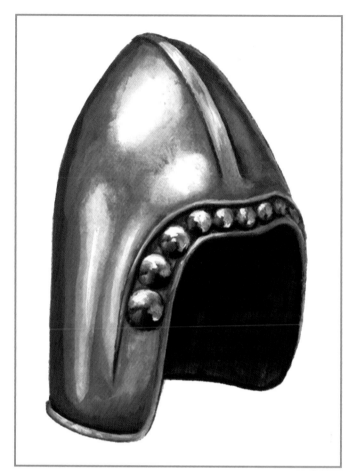

West Highlands of Scotland -1400 to 1600

In the West Highlands of Scotland, where the Lords of the Isles ruled, opposing armies used the landscape more like guerrilla fighters, with hit and run tactics. This was more appropriate to the mountainous terrain they fought in, and their armor, as depicted on many monumental effigies, reflects this. They usually wore a simple conical basinet, sometimes decorated with scalloped borders, with attached aventail of mail. Their body armor consisted of the vertically quilted aketon, which could be covered in pitch to strengthen and waterproof it. Images of this armor have sometimes been wrongly interpreted as evidence of the first Scottish kilts. This armor, together with the heater shield, sword, and spear, remained the most used equipment in the Highlands for many years.

Left: Reconstruction of a West Highland warrior based upon the 14th-century effigy of Bricius MacKinnon at Iona, Scotland. He wears a basinet with attached mail aventail, gauntlets, and a padded aketon, "a linen garment manifoldly sewed and painted or daubed with pitch." His shield is of "heater" form.

Far left: Around the face opening of his basinet is a band of circular studs.

THE WEIGHT AND COST OF ARMOR

In many Hollywood and British films armor is misrepresented as being incredibly heavy, knights being shown winched up by pulleys onto their steeds ("Henry V", 1945). Armor had to be functional and efficient, or it would not have been used. Armor was flexible, and light. A mail hauberk could weigh about 30lbs (13kg). A full Italian armor of the mid-late 15th century weighed around 60-70lbs (27-32kg). This may sound a considerable weight, but it compares extremely favorably with the average of 112lbs (50kg) full kit carried during the First World War (1914-18), and the 120lbs (55kg) carried by British marines in the Falklands War (1982). What is more, the wearer would have been trained daily in the wearing of armor, from perhaps as young as eight years of age. The weight of the armor was distributed all over the body, so it is not surprising to read of armored knights being able to run, lie down, rise up, and even leap into the saddle of a horse unaided. Henry V is just one of many knights reputed to have been capable of this dynamic feat:

> I saw young Harry- with his beaver on,
> His cuisses on his thighs, gallantly arm'd,
> Rise from the ground like a feathered Mercury,
> And vaulted with such ease into his seat,
> As if an angel dropp'd down from the clouds,
> To turn and wind a fiery Pegasus,
> And witch the world with noble horsemanship.
> (Shakespeare, Henry IV, Part 1, IV. 1)

The real problem with armor was not its weight but the way it trapped heat. Body heat resulting from battle exertion could prove fatal. At the Battle of Agincourt (1415) the Duke of York seems to have died of a heart attack brought on by the "heat of battle."

Horse armor was not unduly heavy either. Plate armor for a horse in the 15th century weighed around 60-70lbs (27-32kg), about the same as that of the rider.

Quality armor was always expensive. Mail took a long time to make, and the iron or steel used was costly. Good-quality plate armor took even longer to produce, as it had to fit the wearer more exactly. Cheaper "off the peg" armor did exist, munition armor for the common foot soldier, but it was neither as effective nor as opulent as that made for the aristocracy. In 1441 Sir John Cressey bought a ready-made Milanese armor, slightly decorated with engraving, for £8 6s 8d. In 1614 the armor for Prince Henry (1594-1612) cost £340, at the top of the range for a custom-built order. By contrast Henry VIII was able to purchase 2,000 Florentine light armors or munition armors at 16 shillings each in 1512.

Some armors could consist of as many as 170 different pieces. In 1452 a Parisian armorer and his three or four assistants required three and a half months to build two jousting harnesses. In the same year another armorer built two armors in three months. Applying decoration, such as gilding, increased the time considerably, perhaps adding two months to production time. Some armors took a year or longer to build. The Adler ("Eagle") garniture, made up of 87 pieces, and built in 1547, cost 1,258 guilders. That was the equivalent of 12 years' pay for a courtier. On top of this the gilding added another 463 guilders. It has been noted that a "Milanese Armor" built for Ferdinand I (1503-64), in 1559, cost 2,400 "Welsche (Italian) Kronen," and that this was the equivalent of a master mason working 59 years, "Saturdays and Sundays included!"

An impression of the Emperor Maximilian visiting his court armorer, Conrad Seusenhofer, in Innsbruck. It is based on a woodcut of about 1515 by Hans Burgkmair, from Der Weisskunig. There are three armorers shown, including Seusenhofer, who is working on a helmet.

Europe - 1500 to 1600

The European armor market was still dominated by the Italians and Germans at the beginning of the 16th century. Styles were, however, influenced by each other, as domestic and export markets continued to demand armors that integrated features from either place. Armor did still fail, catastrophically in some cases. At a joust in Paris in 1504, de Maugiron struck Supplanville such a blow that the lance went clean through his body and he fell dead. At the Battle of Pinkie in 1547, Sir Thomas Darcy was luckier: He *was struck glancing on the right side with a bullet of one of the field pieces, and thereby his body bruised with the bowing in of his harness.*

The most identifiable style of German armor in the early 16th century was that known as Maximilian, which lasted for about 30 years. It was named after the Emperor Maximilian (1459-1519), "the last of the knights," who supposedly created the style. Although this is probably not the case, it is known that Maximilian was interested in armor, and in 1504 he set up a court workshop in Innsbruck, which would stay in existence into the 17th century.

In Maximilian armor nearly all the surfaces were covered with regular fluting (apart from the greaves), the ribs being closer together in later examples, and sometimes interspersed with embossed scale decoration. The corrugations not only added a decorative element, but also appear to have given the armor greater strength, and channeled or guided weapon points from vital areas. The turned-over edges of the armor were decorated with a pattern known as "roping," owing to its similarity to twists of rope. Horse armor was also decorated in this manner. Many Maximilian armors were built with mitten gauntlets, a style that covered the fingers with a larger plate, doing away with the need for individual lames to protect the fingers.

Although Italian armors generally remained rounder, they also included the use of fluting, particularly in a spray pattern on the breastplate. Gauntlets were also of the mitten form.

Armors from both areas also began to ape the fashions of the German 16th-century foot-soldiers, the Landsknechte. Their typical slashed and puffed garments were mimicked in steel. Landsknechte themselves wore armor such as a steel head cap and a breast-and back-plate, together with arm defenses. The arm defenses could be in the form of "a pair of splints." They were a form of one-piece vambrace that protected the outside of the arm. The back of the hand was protected by a large plate that was attached to the lower cannon by a turning-pin, which slotted into a slit. Sometimes they wore a deep cape of mail armor, known as a "Bishop's mantle," which gave additional protection to their neck and shoulders. Even contemporary footwear fashions were copied, and the so-called "bear paw" sabatons, which had broad rounded toe plates, reflected the contemporary slashed and splayed shoes. Made-to-measure armor often used the wearer's garments as a pattern. In 1512 a jacket and hose of the 12-year-old Prince Charles, later Charles V(1500-58) were sent to Konrad Seusenhofer to serve as a guide.

Three-quarter armor, extending to the knees and worn with leather boots instead of greaves, became increasingly popular with light cavalry from the mid-16th century. Occasionally only the upper portions of an armor were worn, together with thigh-length boots. Towards the end of the 16th century long laminated tassets, of 14 lames or more, tended to be worn. Breastplates were generally globular at the beginning of the 16th century. This slowly changed until by 1540 a ridge ran down the center of the breastplate, and a pronounced dip had appeared at the middle of the waist, giving it a "long-bellied" appearance. By the 1560s this had become a prominent point, and was a reflection of the fashionable peasecod doublet worn in civilian life, which gave its name to this form of breastplate.

The most obvious influence of fashion is to be found in the late 16th-century "waistcoat cuirass," which was made in the form of the popular peasecod doublet. It was made in two halves, hinged down the back and fastened at the front by button-like studs.

During the mid-16th century so-called "black and white" armor appeared. This was armor covered in black paint, except for panels along the edges, which were left bright. Although this may have begun as an anti-rusting technique its decorative quality was soon acknowledged. It is known that armor for sea service was painted black, as an account from 1546 includes payments for painting armor as *"by reason of the salt water they will by no means be kept clean except they be blackened."*

In the 1520s the cod-piece (or brayette) appeared. This bowl-like padded groin defense was made from one piece, and was detachable, to allow the riding of horses as well as urination. It became fashionable for them to be very prominent and large.

Foot-soldiers wore brigandines or jacks. Brigandines were made from hundreds of small overlapping plates of iron, attached by rivets to a canvas foundation and then covered with a textile. This produced a flexible body armor. Some were covered in velvets, and the more expensive had gilt rivet heads, which formed decorative patterns. Brigandines could be proofed against larger crossbows. Jacks were constructed from small iron or horn plates, or discs, stitched together in between two layers of canvas. The stitching resulted in a criss-cross trellis like pattern. Sometimes these too were covered in richer fabrics. Jacks had been in use in the 15th century and would continue in use, in places like Scotland, until the early 17th century.

Armors were still padded, using horsehair, carded wool, and straw, and lined. Between 1519 and 1523 various pieces of armor made for Henry VIII, including helmets and collars, were lined with yellow and crimson satin. Arming doublets could be made of deerskin or other hide. After about 1570 some armors were decorated with small scallop-shaped leather fabric tabs. Often covered in velvet and riveted to the edges of plates, such as the pauldrons, they reduced the noise of armor plate moving over armor plate. These were known as pickadils or piccadills. They remained in use until the second half of the 17th century. The word itself is

A German Landesknecht of about 1530. He has "splint" arm defenses with projecting plates over the back of the hand. He also wears a "Bishop's mantle" of mail over his shoulders.

first recorded in 1607, and gave its name to a London street where they were made and sold - Piccadilly.

In about 1510 the close helmet was introduced. It would supersede the armet, sallet, and other types of helmet by about the 1520s. The close helmet was made with the vizor and bevor pivoted at the same point, on either side of the head. To put the helmet on, both this section and the skull were swung apart, raising it above the brow, and the helmet was then put over the head. Both sections were then closed together, held in place securely by an integral spring stud, enclosing the head. Once closed the vizor could be raised independently of the bevor. Vizors worn up allowed extra ventilation, and needed not be lowered until the last possible moment. The vizors stayed up by friction, although sometimes small fork-like attachments were used to hold them up. Until about 1530 helmets were often made with a vizor that was stepped, a so-called "bellows" vizor. By the 1540s helmet vizors were often made in two parts. The upper half contained the eye slits, the prow-shaped lower half ("lower bevor") the

"breaths." The vizor sat in the space between the skull and the top of the "lower bevor," both of which, like the single-piece vizor, were pivoted to either side of the helmet. Other forms of helmet that appeared at this time include the open-faced burgonet. A descendant of the sallet, its rounded skull sported a wide peak, or fall, to help protect the face. From about 1525 hinged cheek-pieces were fastened by laces, or a pin, at the chin. It could be worn with a buffe, a full face-defense that could be attached to the sides of the helmet. From the 1520s they were often made of a series of articulated lames, which could be lowered independently, to give better ventilation. This form was known as a falling buffe.

Towards the end of the 16th century simpler forms of helmet appeared. Morions and cabassets were descendants of the medieval kettle-hat or chapel-de-fer. They were lined, and tied under the chin, and often had plume holders. They were much favored by musketeers and archers as the open face was more convenient when taking aim, and consequently stayed in general use until about 1620, when they were replaced by hats. All the finer examples of these helmets were made from one piece of steel, and the finest were decorated to various degrees. The morion was an open-faced helmet, with a broad rim running around its edge, with cheek-pieces. Another variant, called the comb morion, appeared about 1550 (and was therefore not worn by Colombus's conquistadors of 1492, despite what is seen in the Hollywood films). It had a down-turned brim and an upturned peak, at front and rear, and cheek-pieces to protect the ears. It was surmounted by a large central "comb" (hence its name). It was used by cavalry, infantry, town-guards, and also for princely bodyguards, such as the Trabenten guard of the Electors of Saxony.

The simple cabasset, or Spanish morion, was a peaked, almond-shaped helmet, terminating in a small rear-pointing stalk at its apex, with a narrow brim, and cheek-pieces.

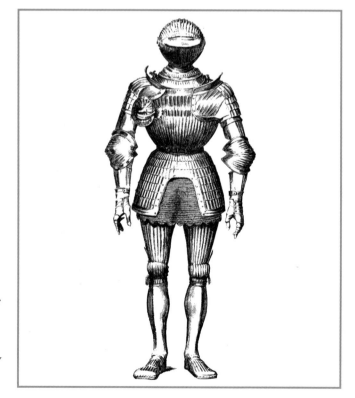

Armor for man in the "Maximilian" style, German, about 1520. The rounded forms with ridges on all parts, except the greaves, are clearly visible.

A comb morion of the Saxon "Trabenten" guard, made in Nuremberg, Germany, about 1580. Of one-piece construction, it would also have had attached cheek-pieces, each made of three plates, on either side.

DECORATION OF ARMOR

Decorated armor has been known for centuries, and predates the classical periods. In the medieval *Song of Roland* one finds descriptions of helmets inlaid with gemstones, such as when Oliver

> *"Strikes Marganice's gold helm on its point,*
> *Bursting away the flowers and the gems,"*

(CXLVI: 1954- 5)

> *"Laces his helmet set with gold and gems"*

(CXXVIII: 3142) -

Armor could also be painted, tinned, silvered, gilded or engraved, not only with pictorial designs, but also with mottoes, usually of a religious nature, such as "AVE MARIA," "AVE DNE" (Ave Domine), "YHS" (Jesus Hominum Salvator), or "JESUS AUTEM TRANSIENS PER MEDIUM ILLORUM IBIT" ('But He passing through the midst of them went His way" - Luke 4:30). These holy sayings were thought to provide the wearer with heavenly protection. Eastern armor could bear floral motifs or calligraphic inscriptions from the Quran. Armor, which was already a significant statement of conspicuous consumption, could be lavishly decorated to make it an even more fabulous symbol of power, wealth, and status. The armor for the three sons of Philip III of Spain (1578- 1621) was particularly spectacular. Even the helmet interiors were silvered. Philip's own helmet had a gilded interior.

Circlets of gold were sometimes worn on helmets, and other circlets, called orles, worn on basinets, could be set with jewels. Armor could also be tinted, that is, heat-blued, and enamelled, for other decorative effects.

One bonus that derived from the decorating of armor, and which had a profound effect on the course of art, was the invention of etching steel plates to make prints. The earliest known etched ornament on armor steel plates seems to be of about 1475, whereas printing from etched plates does not occur until the 16th century.

England - 1511 to 1600

The production of armors on the European continent was superior, both in quantity and quality, to that made in England, where there were only a few armor-making centers. Orders were mostly sent abroad, whether for knightly armor or a large number of munitions armor. In 1512, for instance, Henry VIII (1491-1547) had to use a Florentine dealer to purchase "2,000 complete harness," and in 1513 he purchased armor for 5,000 foot-soldiers from Milan. Copying Maximilian, who had set up his own court workshop, which provided rich gifts to other monarchs, Henry VIII set up his own royal armory in Greenwich, near London. In 1511 he brought a team of Belgian and Italian armorers to Southwark to work for him, and in 1515 he brought 11 "almains" (German and Dutch) armorers to join them in setting up the Greenwich Armouries. This group of armorers successfully created the Greenwich style, which had distinctive features, such as large pauldrons. The style was eclectic and included Italianate cuirasses and Germanic helmets. Greenwich would continue building armors until about 1649.

Originally the Greenwich Armouries produced only for the king, but later, under royal warrant, they made armors for English nobles. Armors made for Henry VIII include one built about 1515-20, for foot combat at the lists. It encased the body entirely, and yet was still flexible. It was so well constructed that 400 years later it was used by NASA to help in the design of moon-walking space-suits for the APOLLO moonshot project of the 1960s and 1970s.

Armors in the 15th century had become more specialized, a different armor being used for a different function; armor made for use in combat or for tournament. In the early 16th century this changed. Multi-role armors were introduced, which could be used for both functions. These armors were built with extra pieces of exchange, which could be swapped and attached, readying the armor for a particular usage. The additional pieces could include defenses for the breastplate, extra thigh defenses, tasset extensions, and different helmets. The whole armor, usually decorated ensuite, was known as a garniture. This idea, which originated in Augsburg, soon spread throughout Europe. The earliest pieces of exchange belong to an armor made in about 1506-10 by Koloman Helmschmid of Augsburg. These garniture armors remained in use until the early 17th century. In 1547 the Adler ("Eagle") garnitur of Ferdinand of Tyrol included a reinforcing 'bullet-proof' breastplate, of 87 pieces that made up the garniture, which could be assembled into three types of tournament armor and five types of field armor.

The anime, an articulated breast and backplate made from separate, overlapping, horizontal plates, riveted together with internal leathers and sliding rivets, first appeared in Italy about 1530. It created a more flexible body. This could also be replaced by a solid breastplate, or by an additional breastplate (attached by a staple in the center of the anime) for tournament. Armor garnitures made at Greenwich were for both field and tournament, and included horse armor. An armor for William, 1st Earl of Pembroke (about 1501-70), of around 1550, is the most complete surviving example. It retains many of the pieces of exchange, including an anime breastplate, reinforcing breastplate, and tasset extensions. Pembroke commanded the English expeditionary force in France in 1557. He may well have worn this armor, or elements of it, that year at the siege of St. Quintin. It is included in an inventory of his home, Wilton House, of 1558.

Other European royal courts followed the example of Maximilian and set up their own armories. The major ones were those of James IV (1473-1513) and James V (1512-42) in Scotland (at Edinburgh, in 1502, and at Holyrood, in 1531), and Gustav Vasa (1496-1560) in Sweden (at Aarboga, in 1551).

At the close of the 16th century it was said that armor was made so massive that "*most men are laden with anvils rather than covered with armor*" (Le Noue, 1575- 90).

In 1590 some men refused to "*wear and carry their armour*' and so it was arranged that '*all soldiers at all musters and trainings shall have over and beside 8d. a day for his wages, a penny a mile for the wearing and carriage of his armor so that it exceed not 6 miles.*"

Armor for William, 1st Earl of Pembroke, and his horse, made in the Greenwich workshop about 1550. Pembroke is shown wearing a burgonet with a falling buffe. He also had additional pieces of exchange, such as a reinforcing breastplate and tasset extensions.

Gun-shield with a breech-loading matchlock pistol, about 1544-47. This is one of some 30 surviving examples probably made for the bodyguard of Henry VIII by Giovanbattista of Ravenna, Italy. Described as "Targetts steilde wt gonne" they are circular, made of wood, and faced with a number of steel plates. The gun barrel passes through the center of the shield, beneath an observation grille.

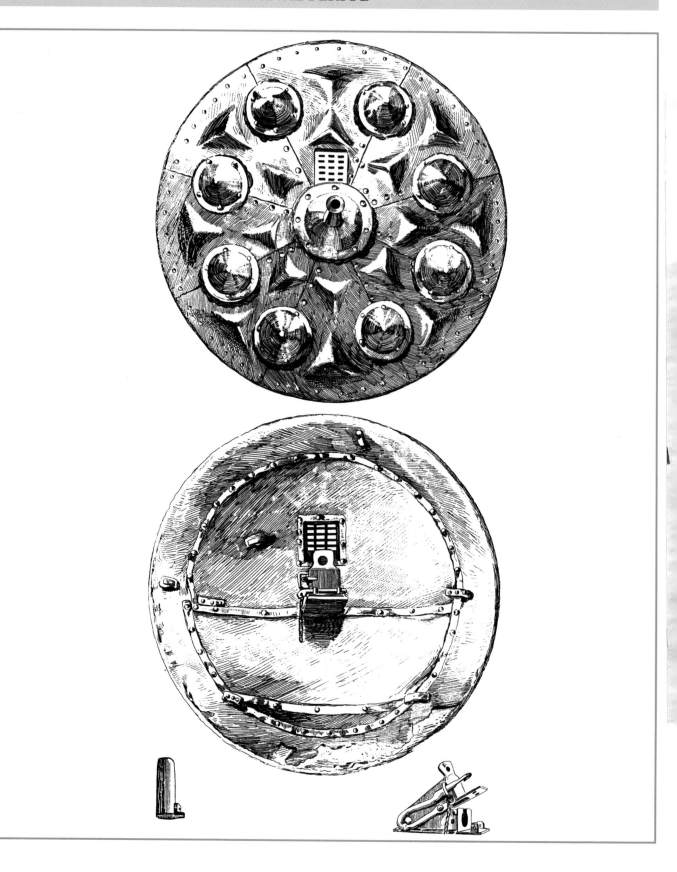

COMBINATION ARMOR

Although armor was used to allow a person to attack with the benefit of protection, it is mostly seen as a defensive tool. Here are a few notable examples of combination armor for attack....

The aboriginal tamarang shield of Australia could also be used as a form of club.

Viking shield rims, sometimes of metal, could be used in a side-swipe or to give a blow to the back of the neck of a downed opponent.

The Scottish targe could have a 12 inch (300 mm) spike screwed into its central boss, to act as a lethal stabbing weapon.

In about 1544-7 some members of the bodyguard of Henry VIII seem to have been equipped with Italian breech-loading matchlock "gonne shields." These were probably originally inspired by drawings of Leonardo da Vinci. Only a few such gun-shields survive, and it is not known how effective they were.

The Indian gauntlet sword, or pata, used by the Mahratta cavalry, was probably wielded like a lance. The hand was slipped into the gauntlet and grasped a bar on the inside, allowing the sword to be thrust at an opponent.

Indians also used a small dual-purpose shield, the madu, held by the left hand. This had two opposed iron-tipped horns attached and could be used both to parry and to stab.

In Germany and Italy, during the late 16th and early 17th centuries, fencing shields were sometimes fitted with lanterns. These "lantern shields" had rings to catch, and possibly break, an opponent's sword blade, and could have various blades or spikes attached to the gauntlet hand grip stabing.

Medieval European gauntlets could be used to deliver savage blows, either with the raised gadlings on the knuckle or the sharp point of the outer cuff, particularly those on "Gothic'"armors. The raised knuckle gadlings were in effect "knuckle-dusters." The "Gothic" armors also had pointed couters on the elbow, which not only looked elegant, but could be used for lashing out with.

"TO DIE IN HARNESS"

The first surviving reference to the word "armor" occurs in 1292. From 1330 armor was also known as harness, and from this term arose the expression "to die in harness," to die in combat, in action.

A hosting harness was another name for field, or battle, armor, hosting meaning battle or encounter.

"And there you could see adjusts of harness"
(**Chauncer,** "The Knight's Tale ," <u>Canterbury Tales</u>.)

"Blow wind Come wrack! At least we'll die with harness on our back"
(Shakespeare, <u>Macbeth</u>.)

The term "suit of armor" is of much later date. It probably originated in the 17th century and was used extensively in the 19th. It would have meant nothing to a medieval knight.

Right: A jousting helm, of "frog-mouth" form, made in south Germany about 1480. This helmet weighs 22lbs8oz (10.23kg). It was worn over a padded lining.

Far right: A tilting helmet made in the Low Countries in about 1500. The combatant leaned forward to see out of the sight near the top of the helmet. The door on the right side could be opened to provide ventilation between contests.

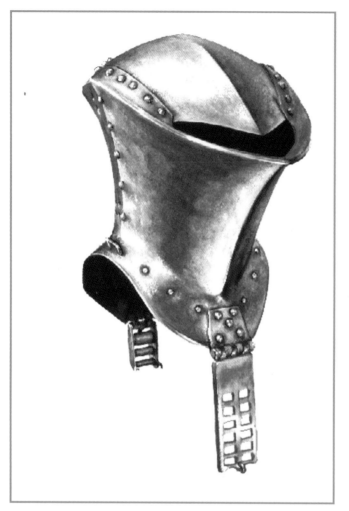

TOURNAMENTS

Another staple of Hollywood medieval epics is the tournament. Tournaments appear to have started out as one-to-one combats between two knights: a continuation of a fabled Trojan tradition. Tournaments provided a form of battle training. To begin with, field armor, and arms were used in these "sham" fights, but as the single combats gave way to mass tournaments, or mêlées, so many knights were either slain or wounded that the tournament games reverted again to single combats, or jousts. In 1130 and 1316 the Church attempted to ban tournaments, with little success.

As the practice of tournaments developed special adaptations in arms and armor were introduced. During the 14th century the barber, an additional plate, was worn over the chest with the hauberk. Saddles were also especially designed with high cantles to protect the legs, and some jousters wore red leg-wear, reputedly to conceal any blood. During the 13th century Jousts of War *(à outrance)*, and Jousts of Peace *(à plaisance)* developed. The former sometimes proved fatal, but seemingly more through accident than intent. Tournament armor was more heavily reinforced than armor for war, making it less mobile but more protective.

The tilt, a wooden barrier, appeared about 1420. It was placed in the tiltyard or lists, where jousts were fought, and it was used to save horse and rider crashing into each other as they charged, left side to left side. The left side of the armors, particularly the elbow area, became increasingly reinforced. Other types of joust included the Gestech (the aim of which was either to unseat one's opponent or to splinter the blunt lance on the specially designed frog-mouth helm, which was in use from the end of the 14th century until the 16th century); and the Rennen (where coronel-headed lances and heavier armor were used). Added thrills for the spectator came from the use of shields, which were spring-mounted to burst asunder, shooting pieces into the air, when struck a blow by the lance. There was also the Scharfrennen (where knights rode at each other with sharp pointed lances).

Horses were also armored, and some wore a *stechkissen*, a padded "fender," on their chests. They usually had their eyes covered with fabric, as it was difficult to make them run at each other.

Tournament armors of this period were heavy: they could weigh up to 90lbs (40kg), and one helmet weighed 20lbs (9kg) alone. Tournaments finished at the close of the 16th century, after which they degraded into displays of flashy equestrian skill, known as the Carousel (which is the origin of the fairground ride), where padded clubs and blunt swords were used to smash opponents' crests.

An armor for a later form of joust, the "Plankengestech," made in Augsburg in about 1590. This form of joust lasted into the 17th century. The armor has a large "manteau d'armes" attached to the bevor.

Foot combat armor made for Henry VIII. It is a tonlet or skirted armor, assembled by his armorers for the Field of the Cloth of Gold in 1520.

Foot combat armor of Henry VIII. This was built at the Greenwich workshop in about 1520, for use at the Field of the Cloth of Gold. It includes steel breeches and cod-piece and encases the body entirely. The "haute-piece" for the right shoulder is missing.

"Puffed and slashed" armor built for Wilhelm von Roggendorf. It was made by Kolman Helmschmid in Augsburg in about 1520.

PARADE ARMORS

Armor was sometimes made primarily for show in the parades and pageants that made up court life. From about 1510 these heavily decorated and embossed armors often included grotesque helmets. These had vizors in the form of human, animal, or bird faces, together with mustaches, horns, and beaks. Probably the most famous is the helmet made by Konrad Seusenhofer as a gift from Maximilian to Henry VIII. The vizor is in the form of a leering caricature portrait of Maximilian himself, together with spectacles and hook nose, from which a dewdrop is suspended.

Until about 1530 "puffed and slashed" armor, copying textile fashions, was also made. The amazing arm defenses of these armors were made up of concentric overlapping lames, with embossed slashes, shaped to appear like puffed sleeves. The bases (the long pleated skirts of the doublet) worn as part of court dress of the period were also copied in steel. The resulting large skirt was made with detachable sections to facilitate horse riding. A related feature, seen in an armor of Henry VIII of about 1520, was the tonlet, a full steel knee-length skirt, which was used in foot-combat tournaments.

From the mid-16th century the interest in the Classical era gave rise to armors made *all'antiqua*, in the style of those worn by Roman emperors and their generals. Burgonets were often used with these armors, because of their similarity to some types of Classical helmets and the fact that the wearer's face could be seen. Round wooden parade shields, painted with scenes from the legends of antiquity, were also produced.

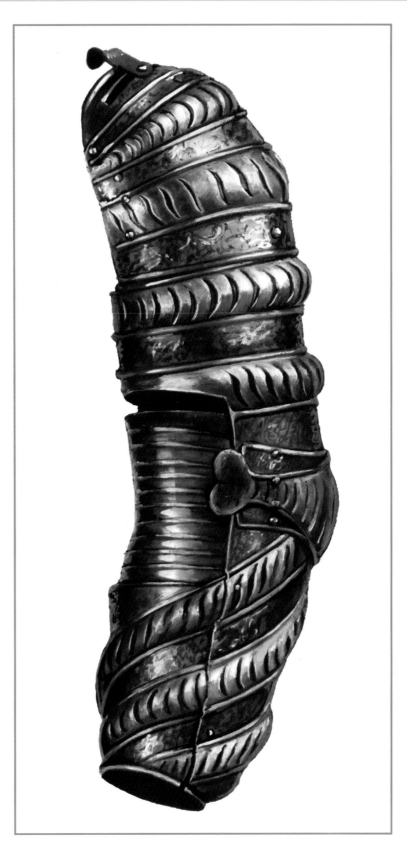

This is the arm defense (vambrace) of a "puffed and slashed" armor of about 1520-25. It is attributed to Kolman Helmschmid. The slashed horizontal bands imitate civilian dress.

ARMOR PRODUCTION CENTERS IN EUROPE

Armor was manufactured in only a few centers. Good-quality raw materials and resources were required for making fine armor, as well as highly specialized skills. These occurred both north and south of the Alps, in southern Germany and northern Italy. It was from the Alps that the water power came to drive the water-driven tools and hammers, which made, shaped, and polished the armor. Italy had been exporting armor since the late 13th century. Armorer's workshops could be found in Brescia, Ferrara, Florence, Genoa, Modena, Mantua, Milan, Venice, Urbino, and Rome and Naples in the south. Milan was the biggest center in Italy.

Germany had two major areas, the region around Cologne (Rhine-Westphalia), and that in south Germany, Nuremberg, Landshut, and Innsbruck.

There were also other smaller centers, at Strasbourg, Ulm, Memmingen, Stuttgart, Vienna, Graz, Basel, Zurich, Leipzig, Erfurt, Magdeburg, and Lübeck. Outside Italy and Germany, the Low Countries produced armor at Bruges, Brussels, and Tournai.

In France armor was produced in Paris and at St. Quentin, Noyon, Senlis, Rouen, Chambly le Hauberger, Montaubon, Tours, and Bourges. At Lyons a Milanese "colony" of armorers was employed. Spain's centers included Barcelona, Valencia, Burgos, Seville, and Eugui. England's only major center was London, though some armor was made in York, in perhaps a particularly "English" style. In Scotland, Edinburgh was a very small center. Sweden produced armor at Aaboga. In Eastern Europe both Prague and Cracow were important centers.

Germany and Italy dominated the market to such a degree that what was the "International" style of armor before the 15th century later became either "Italian" or "German"- style armor.

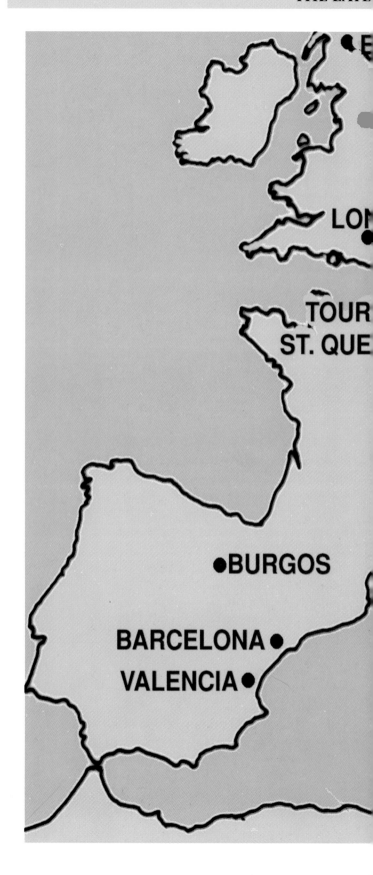

RGH

BRUGES
●BRUSSELS

●PRAGUE

●COLOGNE

RIS   ●CRACOW

●
NURENBERG

LYONS

●INNSBRUCK

●BRESCIA

IILAN●

●VENICE
IOA●   ●FERRARA

MANTUA   MODENA

FLORENCE   ●URBINO

●
ROME

NAPLES

The map shows the main production centers. Other sites mentioned in the text are smaller local manufactories and thus, with the exception of Edinburgh, are not shown.

A harquebusier's "pott" of the 1640s, possibly made in the Netherlands. It was imported into England for use by Royalist forces loyal to Charles I. It has a single sliding nasalbar to protect the front of the face.

Europe - 1600 to 1700

In the 17th century wars erupted throughout Europe. A combination of politics and religion led to the Thirty Years' War (1618-48) and the "English" Civil War (1642-51), among others. The power and effectiveness of firearms had increased, and armor became less efficient at protecting its wearer from injury. To counter the power of musket balls armor had to be made thicker. This also made it heavier and more uncomfortable to wear. Armor could be tested, or "proved," against musket ball, shot at close range. The many musket ball marks on armor of this period were made in this way, rather than in battle. Armor that successfully defeated a ball was known as "armor of proof." (This was not a new idea, as 15th-century armor had been tested against cross-bows.)

Armor, particularly for the infantryman, became more concentrated around the vital parts of the body, the head, and torso. The heavy cavalryman (known as a cuirassier after 1620), still clinging to older ideas of equestrian rank, as well as practicalities, tended to wear knee-length, three-quarter armor with tassets. In the English Civil War Sir Arthur Haselrig raised a regiment of heavy cavalry for Parliament. Exceptionally they wore full armor, and as a result were known as "Haselrig's Lobsters." This armor apparently saved Haselrig's life at the Battle of Roundway Down (1643). However, contemporary writings allude to what some soldiers felt about being summoned to a muster *"as a cuirassier in russet armes."*

"It will kill a man to serve in a whole cuirass. I am resolved to use nothing but back, brest and gauntlet. If I had a pott for the hedd that were pistol-proofe, it may be I would use it, if it were light, but my whole helmett will be of noe use to mee at all."
(Sir Edmund Verney, letter, 1639)

Verney did gain a "pott," but finding that it did not fit, he used it instead to make porridge!

Those wearing only a collar and breast -and back-plates sometimes wore an arm defense to protect the rein arm, an elbow-length bridle gauntlet.

Pikemen, in the infantry, wore collar, breast-and

Armor worn by pikemen who fought on both the Royalist and Parliamentarian sides during the English Civil War. It consisted of a simple helmet, or "pott," usually made from two pieces, a gorget, a breast -and back -plate, and a pair of tassets.

backplates, long wide tassets, and a pot, a brimmed helmet, weighing about 3lbs (1.4kg). Armor of this sort was also used in the colonies, being found in places in the Americas, such as Jamestown (1607).

Beneath these armors, and often in their place, the soldiers wore buff coats. They were made from thick leather and could turn sword cuts, although musket balls at close range could inflict fatal wounds. Gustavus II Adolphus (1594-1632) died at the battle of Lutzen, when a ball penetrated his elk-hide buff coat. Gauntlets were also made from buff leather. Buff coats were often worn with a steel collar.

Silk body armor was tried out in the late 17th century. A top layer of silk covered wadding with a stiff backing, such as leather. Purportedly pistol proof, its success is debatable. As a later commentator noted, it

"was as safe as in an House, for it was impossible anyone could go to strike him for laughing"
(Roger North, *Examen*, 1740).

The close helmet remained in use until the mid-17th century, although other helmet forms were used. The Zischagge was a helmet used in Eastern Europe (Poland and Hungary) from about 1550. It had a bowl-like skull, with a wide laminated neck-guard, cheek-pieces, and a fixed or pivoted fall. A sliding nasal bar running down through the fall protected the face. The open-faced, English pot was a form of Zischagge, which tended to be used by the cavalry, and weighed about 5.5 lbs (2.5kg). In these the facial area was protected from a slashing sword cut, aimed to the face, by vertical triple bars attached to the peak of the helmet. They had neck-guards, which on more expensive pieces were laminated, and ear flaps. The neck-guard gave rise to their modern name, the "lobster tailed pot."

Helmets were also made in the shape of civilian hats, but out of steel instead of leather or textile, some with a sliding nasal bar to protect the face. Charles I (1600-1649) is said to have worn a steel hat covered with black velvet at the Battle of Naseby (1645). Steel skull caps, or collapsible secretes, could also be worn beneath normal civilian headgear.

Siege armors were worn by sappers involved in dangerous mining or trench operations. These consisted of thicker and heavier helmet, breast-and-backplates, together with a very heavy triple-barred pot, which was actually supported on the shoulders. Other siege helmets had large brims, front and rear.

In the mid-17th century standing armies began to be raised, clad in uniforms rather than armor. Remaining elements of armor slowly atrophied, the breast-and- backplates being worn only by the mounted cuirassiers. Gradually the armorer's skills declined. Helmets that were previously constructed from one piece of steel were now often made from two halves joined together along the comb. Full or three-quarter armor tended to be relegated to the artist's studio where victorious generals had their portraits painted in armor, aspiring to echo the paragons of knightly chivalry and combat.

The Scottish shield, the targe, or target, which derived from the medieval bucklers (if not the shields of the Vikings), was still used against troops armed with firearms. It was constructed from two-ply wood doweled and glued together. The exterior was covered in leather, often tooled, and decorated with metal edging and studs. The interior was covered in deer or cattle hide. A murderous spike could be attached to the central metal boss, and so turn a defensive parrying device into an offensive weapon. A notable incident involving the use of a targe occurred during the battle of Killiecrankie (1689) when an English government soldier used a sword to attack a Scot. His blows fell ineffectually on the Scotsman's targe, driving him to exclaim, *"You dog. Come out from behind that door and fight like a man!"*

WORDS AND TERMS DERIVING FROM ARMOR AND ITS USAGE

Aegis: Protection, a shield.
The shield of Zeus in Greek mythology. It was covered in goatskin and bore the head of the gorgon Medusa. Renaissance pageant shields were also painted with a gorgon's face, possibly in emulation of this.

Carrying one's heart on one's sleeve: Showing one's loyalty or allegiance.
During tournaments a knight would often bear a "favor" from his lady, in the form of a ribbon or veil, which was tied around one of his arms.

Chink in the armor: Fissure or gap.
This refers to weak spots in an armor, such as the gaps where the arms meet the body.

Crestfallen: Disheartened, dispirited.
Sometimes crests might droop and look woeful. Also in certain tournaments, such as mêlées and the later carousels, competitors tried to knock off, or smash, opponents' crests with blunted swords or clubs. The one who retained his crest at the end was the winner.

Gauntlet, run the: Risk danger.
During the Thirty Years' War Germans adopted a Swedish military punishment, in which the miscreant had to run between two facing rows of soldiers, who struck him as he passed. This could prove fatal. The passage, or gatlopp in Swedish, in German became gantlope. This was corrupted to gantlet, or gauntlet.

Gauntlet, fling, or throw, down the: To give challenge.
The act of throwing down the gauntlet to challenge a foe to combat can be traced back to at least the mid-16th century, and has remained in use ever since:
"I cast down my gauntlet, take it up who dares""
(Thomas Nash, Pasquil's *Apologie*, 1590)

Knight in shining armor: Term of derision, meaning a person of great promise but likely to disappoint.
Although on first appearance this may appear a compliment, it is usually a term of derision, referring to a knight with bright armor, as one unbesmirched by combat in the field.

Mailed fist; iron hand: Threat of force.
This phrase may date back only to the 19th century, but its actual origin lies in the mail armor worn in the earlier European medieval period. Iron hands were early prosthetic devices, built in the 16th century, often by armorers.

Panache: Showiness, or swagger.
Originally the word panache applied to crests of feathers on Renaissance helmets and chaffrons. The feathers were often brightly dyed and appeared highly extravagant. Ostrich feathers were used as they allegedly remained unruffled by the wind. Henry VIII once appeared armed and on horseback with a great panache *"that came down to the arson of his sadel."*

Panoply: A complete armor.
Meaning a complete harness, as well as a display or collection of armor, panoply derives from the Greek Panoplia (Pan- all, and Hopla- armor), and has been in use from at least 1632.

Raise one's hat; salute: Greet.
This harks back to the days when knights wore close helmets with vizors, which were raised to allow recognition and greeting.

Stretch a point: To go further than strict rules allows.
Points were laces that attached pieces of armor to the arming doublet. If they became loose or stretched, after being tied, they could disable the armor during combat.

Japan - 5th century to 1800

The early native armor, the tanko, of 5th-8th-century Japan, was made up of iron plates, some of large size. It seems to have been replaced by the lamellar armor of the Asiatic mainland of iron scales laced with leather thongs. This was developed by the Japanese into the keiko ("hanging armor") and used by their mounted warriors. Horse armor in the form of iron chaffrons had been introduced to Japan in the 5th or 6th century.

By the close of the Heian period (1185) the great armor, the oyoroi (so called because of the size of its larger components), had developed. It was worn by nobles such as the mounted samurai archers. The oyoroi consisted of various pieces including the do, or cuirass, which wrapped around the body and had a separate defense for the right side. Plaited silk was used for lacing the hundreds of small plates in the rest of the armor, rather than leather, and this made the whole a rigid, yet flexible form. The colored lacing braids, the odoshige, secured the plates, made up of rows of laced scales, together. The iron plates were covered in layers of black lacquer, which made the armor waterproof and rot-proof. The infantry wore the simpler domaru ("body round") form of armor, which had rows around the body overlapping under the right arm.

After the Mongol invasions of the 1270's nobles fought on foot and also wore the domaru together with the helmet, shoulder, and leg elements of the oyoroi. Lacquered mail armor was also used, particularly from the Nanbokucho period (1336-1392).

In Japan it was the rich and powerful aristocratic warrior class, the buke (of which the samurai, meaning "one who serves," were one grade), who wore the finest armor. To a degree they resembled the knights of Western Europe, in that they also followed a military code of honor, bushido. They dominated the battlefield and state politics from the 12th century until their abolition in 1868, when the Emperor was re-established as ruler after an almost 900-year gap.

The finest examples of the craft of the Japanese armorer are found during the Muromachi period (1333-1568), when the oyoroi was still being worn by the highest ranks. Varied forms of helmet, or kabuto, were used, and included attachments such as a peak, the mabisashi, and grotesque half-face masks, mengu, with frightening expressions and often large mustaches. Other helmets had a hole, the tehen, at their apex. This not only gave some ventilation, but allowed the samurai's short queue of hair (motodari) to pass through. A cap, the eboshi, was worn beneath the helmet, and provided some padding, together with the wearer's hair. Helmet linings, ukebari, appeared during the Kamakura and Nanbokochu periods (1185-1392). The helmet bowl, or hachi, made of riveted plates, protected the skull, while the face was protected by a one-piece brow and cheek-guard, the happuri, which was tied behind the head, under the helmet. A tapering laminated neck-guard, the shikoro, reached to the shoulders, and decorated upswept plates at the side of the helmet, fukigaeshi, added to its defense from arrow shot and sword slash. The throat was protected by the yodarekake, which was attached to the mengu.

Many armors included distinctive large rectangular shoulder defenses, osode, made up of rows of lamellar armor. The left arm was protected by an armored silk sleeve, the kote, made from a combination of mail and plate, which was worn laced around the chest. The right arm was left free to allow maximum flexibility, although later the right arm was also protected, as well as the left, by armored sleeves, the shinogote, which used splints on the forearm.

Lower body and thigh defenses, the kusazuri, made up of four plates of scale, were suspended from the do. Later shin-guards of small plates, suneate, were

Helmet and upper part of Japanese armor of a 19th-century reproduction of the Muromachi period (1333-1568) oyoroi. It was presented to Queen Victoria.

used. Hands were gloved and fur-covered shoes (kutsu) were worn on the feet.

Most foot soldiers and retainers wore the domaru or the simpler and lighter cuirass, the haramaki ("belly wrapper"), which wrapped around the body and fastened down the center of the back. From the 14th century the haramaki was also worn by the samurai. Their kusazuri were of seven or eight sections to allow greater mobility on foot, and they wore straw sandals. Later foot soldiers could also carry a large wooden shield, the tate, similar to a Western pavise.

Japan was gripped by civil war throughout the Sengoku or Warring States period (1467-1568). Although gilded crests had appeared on helmets during the late Heian or Fujiwara period (894-1185), large and fantastic crests, tate mono, now became common. These were sometimes in the form of animals, and could be made from stag antlers, buffalo horns, or lacquered leather and wood. Generals could wear decorated horns of thin gilded iron or copper plates (kuwagata), and crests worn on the front of the helmet were known as maedate. Such crests were not the only form of heraldry used. Armor itself could be decorated with a family badge, the mon, which identified the user, as did the banner, the sashimono, carried on a bamboo staff set in brackets on the back of the cuirass. Different colored lacquers on the armor plates also added to the spectacle of the battlefield at this time.

The immense amount of combat also led to an increased demand for armor for the common soldier. The tatamido was made from mail and plate, sewn on to a fabric foundation, and could be folded. It was cheaper, quicker to produce, more portable, and easier to store in bulk, than traditional styles. It also had the added advantage that it could be laced more simply. The traditional form of armor was found wanting during the prolonged campaigns that were fought through the seasons. In the summer heat the armor could become uncomfortably hot to wear, and in the winter the lacing was:

"Liable to freeze…on long and distant campaigns it becomes evil smelling and overrun by ants and lice, with consequent ill-effects on the health of the wearer. It is also easily damaged because it will retain a spear instead of letting it glide off harmlessly"
(Sakakibara Kozan, *Chukokatchu Seisakuben*)

The Portuguese, who were the first Europeans to contact Japan, in either 1542 or 1543, introduced firearms. After this some Japanese heavy plate armor was made musket-ball-proof, although it was never popular as it reduced mobility.

During the Edo period (1603-1868) nobles used armors that included embossed and archaic features. By the close of the 18th century accurate copies of old armors were being made, and genuine older pieces were being refurbished. Armor was made by groups, or schools, of armorers (katchushi), though some family dynasties of makers did exist. It was only in the 19th century that the use of armor was discontinued and Western-style uniforms were worn instead.

A Samurai wearing armor laced with leather (kawaodoshi) rather than with silk. Leather was prone to hardening and shrinkage if it got wet too often, so silk was more commonly used.

The Americas -1500 to 1800

When Columbus (1451-1506) reached the Americas in 1492, his accompanying armed forces and those who followed wore the same equipment as that found in many other European countries, particularly those of Spain and Portugal. Mail and plate armor were both used, mail being used into the 17th century. Sallets, bevors, and (later on) burgonets and comb morions would have been worn on the head. Brigandines and breast-and back-plates would have protected the torso. Fragments of scale armor have been found in New Mexico, which indicate that such armor was also being used during the 16th century, if not later. When Cortes (1485-1547) invaded what is now Mexico in 1519 eleven out of 550 men wore extensive plate armor.

Little survives of Amerindian armor, though its appearance can be reconstructed from the use of surviving pottery figurines and illustrated codices. Aztecs wore the ichcahuipilli, a thickly padded, short-sleeved, knee-length, cotton jacket and padded helmets. Aztec nobility used a form of heraldry, based on animals that symbolized courage. A warrior could attain one of two "military orders," that of "Jaguar knight," or "Eagle knight." The armor of the former was covered in the tight- fitting fur of jaguars, the animal's head forming the headdress. The helmets of the latter were made in the form of eagle heads and used the feathers of eagles, the wearer's face peering out of the open "beak." Their shield, the chimalli, was often decorated with an elaborate feather mosaic in geometric patterns.

The conquistadors were usually equipped with helmet, body armor, and shield. The shields were often of the Spanish form known as the adarga. This heart-shaped form originated with the Moors of Africa and continued in use from the 13th to the18th century. In the humid conditions of South America, however, much of the European steel armor was prone to rust. Despite anti-rusting techniques such as painting and tinning, it still disintegrated. This, together with the heat, persuaded many soldiers to wear leather cuirasses or the effective quilted cotton armors of their opponents. Heredia's Colombian expedition chose *"cotton for defensive armor, the moisture not being suitable for cuirasses."*(Cieza de Leon, *Chronicle of Peru*).

Although apparently more comfortable to wear, it is recorded that during the conquest of Mexico some men were disabled by pains in the groin caused by this *"cotton armor that they wore day and night."* However, such problems pale into insignificance when compared to those of some soldiers in Florida in 1543 who fell into water and *"with the weight of their armour, sunke down to the bottome."* Richer horsemen seem likely to have worn three-quarter steel armors, probably with open-faced helmets. Of course it was the use of the firearm and horse, rather than a specific form of armor, that enabled the conquistadors to conquer South and Central America.

In North America full body armor was rare, but some armor pieces were made from hides of animals such as moose or caribou. The hides could be sewn,or glued together. The Plains Indians used buffalo hide to make shields. Alaskan people on the north-west coast were influenced by Asian and European contact to make cuirasses from slats of wood covered in sealskin, which wrapped around the body, and also hide armor reinforced with Chinese coins. They were in use in the 18th century.

Reconstruction of an Aztec "Jaguar" knight of the 16th century. The normal quilted cotton cuirass was worn beneath jaguar skin, which denoted a high rank. The spears and swords are edged with sharp slivers of black obsidian.

The Near East, Central and South Asia

Armor of similar type was used throughout the Indo-Persian and Islamic world, including Turkey. The Mughals introduced Persian forms of armor to India. This mainly consisted of a combination of butted mail shirts and plate defenses. The cuirass, char' aina ("four mirrors" in Persian), consisted of four slightly curved rectangular plates, for the chest, sides, and back, which could be linked to each other by mail or worn over a mail shirt. Arms were defended by hinged plates, dastana, which encased the whole lower arm, and hands by mail gloves. Mail was often decorated by the inclusion of rows of brass links to create geometric patterns. Quilted armor, known since the classical period in India, was also worn by both Hindus and Muslims and remained in use until the 19th century, when it was claimed to be bullet-proof.

The most common form of helmet in India was the conical steel top, similar to the Persian kulah. It had sliding nasal bars, mail neck defenses, and usually a spiked finial on top. Persian kulah could have a number of sliding bars protecting the face and had crest holders for plumes of peacock feathers, for instance. The round steel Indian and Persian shield, dhal or sipar, usually had a central boss surrounded by a number of smaller bosses.

Most of this armor was decorated, often using the koftgari technique in which the steel surface is incised or hatched, and layers of gold are applied.

Armor of mail and plate, including coat (zereh bagtar) and helmet (kolah zereh). Indian, Mughal, early 17th century.

98

Armor for Elephant, Indian, probably early 17th century. It is thought to have been captured by Clive of India at the Battle of Plassey (1757).

Oceania

With the great voyages of discovery and exploration, the West came upon different cultures in the Pacific Ocean, many of which had evolved their own unique forms of body armor, using naturally occurring materials. Perhaps the best known are the armors from the Gilbert Islands. The body defense was made from woven coconut fibers. A looser weave could cover the arms and legs, but the cuirass was much stronger and included a high rear neck-guard. The helmet was made from the spiny skin of the pufferfish. This armor protected the wearer from the swords and spears developed in the islands, which were studded with shark teeth.

Armor worn by people from the Gilbert Islands in the Pacific Ocean. This armor was made from coconut fiber and fish skin. They fought with swords and spears edged with sharks' teeth.

Mongolia

In 1206 Temujin (1167-1227), better known as Genghis Khan, embarked upon the building of his empire. Peking fell to him in 1215. From surviving descriptions it appears that armor was worn by only a few of the Mongols. It was made mostly from stiffened leather. Occasionally iron was also used, in the form of mail hauberks and plate. Mongol armor protected the arm to the elbow and reached below the knee, opening down the front for easy horse riding. It is not clear whether the armor protected the back as well as the front. Sharkskin may have been used as a form of veneer on some armors. Oxhide leather, in cuir-bouilli form, was joined together to make a flexible plate armor and was waterproofed with coats of pitch.

Lamellar armor was made by lacing small pierced iron plates together with leather thongs and binding these strips into larger plates. Giovanni da Pian del Carpini, a papal ambassador to the Mongols between 1245-47, noted that the armor was *"so highly polished that a man may mirror his face in it."*

Helmets were worn, some of which had central spikes, others plumes. Carpini also describes lamellar horse armor, made of five sections, used together with a chaffron.

Mongols of the 13th century wore similar lamellar armor to this Tibetan cavalry armor of the 17th to 19th centuries.

Africa

Since the 15th century the expanding empires of the West European nations brought contact and conflict with the peoples of Africa. The art of some African kingdoms includes images of the European soldiers who made contact. Sixteenth-century Portuguese soldiers are depicted on many Benin (Nigeria) bronzes. Shields of different types were in use all over the continent, from shields made of crocodile and hippopotamus hide in the Sudan, to the oval cowhide shield, the ishilangu, of the Zulu in the south. A few Zulu regiments carried shields with the very distinctive colors and markings of cowhide. The Zulu shields were leaf-shaped, decorated by two parallel lines of hide lacings down the center, with a wooden grip at the rear.

Body armor was fairly rare. In northern Nigeria the Bornu used a form of multicolored quilted cotton armor, for both man and horse, which in appearance looks almost like that of a European medieval knight. In North Africa mail shirts were sometimes worn, and in the Sudan distinctive patched and embroidered cloth coats (jibbahs), became a uniform of the armies of the Mahdist revolt, finally defeated at the Battle of Omdurman (1898).

British tropical helmet for other ranks, colonial volunteers, about 1905. With its high crown and broader brim, this is very similar to the "Wolseley" pattern that replaced the British Army's foreign service tropical helmet in 1904.

AFRICAN ARMOR

In the Sudanese desert in the early morning of September 5, 1898, an army of 60,000 Mahdist fundamentalists launched itself at the guns of an Anglo-Egyptian force positioned outside the town of Omdurman.

Many of the Mahdists wore chain mail over the characteristic linen smock, the jibbeh. Others wore quilted armor made of thick quilted cotton stuffed with kapok.

These were "medieval armors" worn by men mostly carrying swords, shields, and spears. They were simply no match for the British and Egyptians armed with bolt-action rifles, artillery, and 44 Maxim machine-guns. Fire was opened at 6.45 a.m. and carried on to 11.30. When the firing stopped 26,000 Mahdists lay dead or wounded. None had got within half a mile of the Anglo-Egyptian line.

A quilted horse and cavalry armor of about 1899, from Sub-Saharan Africa. The garments are made of cotton stuffed with kapok, while the horse also has a decorative nose plate of brass or tin. While they were a suitable defense against arrows, such magnificent armors were useless against the British machine-guns at the Battle

A British yeomanry officer's helmet of the leather "Tarleton" pattern, c. 1820. Leather helmets for light cavalry were introduced into the British Army after their successful use by Loyalist forces in the American War of Independence in the 1770s.

Europe -1700 to 1914

Warfare in the 18th century was said to be the time of "lace-trimmed war." Certainly armor was little used compared to previous centuries. In 1706-07, during the Wars of the Spanish Succession, 900 troopers were issued with breastplates, proofed against shot. This was a rare occurrence: elsewhere armor was often relegated to a less martial use. For instance in 1720 the armories at the Tower of London included 72 helmets to be converted into "caps for Firemen."

The cuirassiers continued to wear breast-and back-plates, although some did away with the backplate altogether. One of the few pieces of armor that survived as a reminder of the earlier full armor was the officer's gorget. This was a crescent-shaped plate suspended around the neck as a throat defense. It offered no real protection but was a symbol of rank. As the 18th century progressed even these shrank in size, and, made of silver or brass, would bear a royal cipher and possibly a regimental device or number.

They were finally discarded by the British Army in 1830.

Helmets, on the other hand, were still seen as effective, particularly by the cavalry, and various forms of helmet, made from leather, brass, and steel, continued in use.

Perhaps more surprisingly, the shield remained in use in some areas of Europe, even against "high-tech" armies. At the Battle of Culloden (1746) many of Charles Edward Stuart's rebel infantry charged towards the British government army with sword and targe. But after proscription even they fell into disuse, Boswell and Johnson noting in their tour of the Scottish Highlands in 1773 that they were used as lids for barrels and churns.

By the 1750s the success of the flintlock musket in the hands of disciplined infantrymen and the continued technical advances of artillery seemed to have made the armored fighting man obsolete. Yet in Central Europe the breastplated cavalryman — the

Left: French cuirassier of the Imperial French Army, 1802-15. There had been an armored cuirassier regiment in the Royal French Army from the 1660s, but it was not until 1802, when Napoleon decided to use his heavy cavalry in the same "shock" role as that pioneeered by Frederick the Great, that his cavalry were reorganized and issued with helmets and breastplates.

Far left: A Prussian cuirassier of the army of Frederick the Great, 1757. Only the front of the breastplate was worn, secured at the back by two cross straps. The head was protected by iron bands sewn into the cavalryman's tricorne hat.

cuirassier – was still to create a powerful symbol of martial prowess and prove decisive on the battlefield for the next 65 years.

The Seven Years' War of 1756-63 witnessed a resurgence of the influence of armored horse, under the direction of King Frederick the Great of Prussia. Realizing that sheer weight and size made his cavalry too slow for rapid maneuver under fire, King Frederick turned these old-fashioned tactical virtues into practical use and deployed his breastplated heavy horse en muraille – in closed ranks, the riders knee to knee, moving forward slowly, inexorably, as an armored mass, then delivering a shock charge at the enemy line from barely 100 yd (90 m).

It was a tactic that was to prove its worth at the Battle of Rossbach in November 1757 when in two charges 38 squadrons of breastplated Prussian cuirassiers (6,000 men), acting with rapidly moving Prussian infantry, routed a combined army of French, Russians, and Austrians in little over 90 minutes. The Prussians lost 548 men, the Allied force 10,150.

The uniform of the Prussian cuirassier was practical, but kept fully with the fashions of the time. On his head was a large black felt tricorne hat reinforced inside with strips of iron sewn into the crown, giving the head some protection from sword blows. Over his shirt he had a waistcoat and buckskin jerkin. His breast plate was of iron and weighed about 32 lbs (14 kg). It was secured tightly across the back by two leather straps fastened crosswise. Only the front plate was worn, the backplate having been taken out of service in the 1740s. While this may seem likely to have compromised the effectiveness of the armour, in sheer practical terms it lightened the load of both rider and horse and emphasized the cuirassier's role as an attacking soldier, always on the offensive. If the man's back was to the enemy, it didn't deserve protection, and he was certainly not going to get it paid for out of the royal purse. Armor cost money, and King Frederick was a practical man.

The regiments of the Prussian Royal Guard (the Garde du Corps) wore a breastplate of "white" burnished iron, while line regiments wore the iron plates in their black unburnished form, which were often also painted black to keep out rust.

To protect their legs in the charge, all Prussian cuirassiers wore characteristic heavy leather riding boots, which extended to a broad 'bucket' shape over the knees.

Interestingly, the Imperial Austrian cuirassiers of the period, though wearing uniforms in the Prussian style, did use a back plate to their armor, though only when fighting the Turks. A heavy lobster-tailed iron helmet was also kept in store for the same enemy, and this complete armored rig was reported to have been worn in action during the Austro-Turkish campaigns of 1788-89.

Conscious of the symbolic significance of armor and its centuries-long history, many of Europe's greatest royal houses, including those in Russia, Sweden, and France, followed Prussia in retaining regiments of breastplated cuirassiers as the sovereign's personal guard, the Garde du Corps. The exception was England, where the civil wars of the seventeenth century had reduced royal power and bred a popular distaste for the sight of armored soldiers on the streets.

In practical terms the 18th century had also seen the English army in an increasing number of overseas campaigns in the harsher climes and rugged terrain of North America and India. The difficulties of wearing armor in these conditions, together with the cost of transporting breastplates by sea over thousands of miles, were making the wearing of plate armor obsolete.

The exceptions to this trend occurred in the case of England's involvement in Europe's conflicts. In 1758, in support of Prussia in the Seven Years' War, the English Royal Horse Guards (the Blues) were ordered to Germany complete with breastplates and skullcaps on the continental model. In 1793 with the outbreak of the French Revolutionary Wars, the Blues were issued with the same armor on their way to the Flanders campaign, though by this time the gear was found to be so old as to be unusable.

Though the Prussians abolished the breastplate in 1790 with the accession of a new king, Frederick William II, another head of state a little over ten years later would see the potential of armored horse on Frederick the Great's model, and exploit it on the battlefield to the utmost.

In post-revolutionary France Napoleon Bonaparte,

like Frederick the Great, had territorial ambitions and was more than willing to use aggressive war to achieve them. From 1802 Napoleon, at the time France's self-proclaimed Consul for Life, ordered that 24 regiments of cavalry be reorganized to create 12 regiments of cuirassiers, beginning with the 8th Cavalry Regiment. The 8th had formerly been the Cuirassiers du Roi of the Ancien Régime before the Revolution and as such had worn breastplates since 1665.

Napoleon's cuirassiers wore both front and back plates of burnished steel, the back plate being the lighter of the two. They were secured by straps of overlapping brass scales at the shoulder and by a leather belt at the waist, which was buckled at the front and secured with rivets at the back. All ranks of cuirassier except trumpeters wore breastplates, even generals, after an imperial order from Napoleon in 1807, though the officers' armor was naturally more ornate, often bearing gilt, ornamental shoulder straps. There were three different patterns of breastplate issued to the regiments from 1802 to 1809.

The distinctive steel cuirassier helmet was first introduced to the 8th Cavalry Regiment in 1800 after its success at the Battle of Hochstaedt in Germany, and was a private purchase by the regiment's commanding general. Based on the dragoon pattern of the time – French dragoons had worn helmets of various types since their inception in the 1660s – the helmet was peaked with a metal comb and chin scales and was decorated with a horsehair crest and a band (or "turban") of black calf skin round the crown. The helmet was adopted by all cuirassier regiments after 1802.

Despite the fact that these pattern helmets with minor alterations have seen continual service in France from that year to this (they are now used by the French Republic's ceremonial mounted honor guard), in 1802 the rank and file troopers looked on the helmet with some disdain. To many it was not prepossessing enough; it displayed too little élan and, what is more, it made them look like dragoons, that lower form of life, which every real cavalryman knew were little more than infantrymen on nags.

Napoleon's other branch of heavy cavalry – the carabiniers – were also issued with breastplates and helmets, but only after the regiments had taken heavy

British Life Guard of the 1820s. King George IV reintroduced breastplates to his Royal guard after his accession in 1820. The adoption of armor was more a fashion statement than a practical exercise, and breastplates and helmets were never worn in combat. The Life Guards' helmet is of the same "Roman" pattern adopted by Napoleon's carabiniers in 1810.

casualties at the Battle of Wagram in 1810. The carabinier helmet was in the popular classically Roman style of the period and was high-crested and peaked and made of yellow metal. The breastplate differed from that of the cuirassier in being covered with thin brass sheeting. The breastplate for carabinier officers was copper-plated.

The sight of these armored regiments en masse was awe-inspiring, as was the intention, and their disciplined squadrons cut a swathe through Napoleon's enemies at such battles as Eylau in 1806 and Leipzig in 1813. The helmets and breastplates themselves, however, though intimidating symbols of martial prowess, proved of limited worth in combat.

In a mêlée of cavalryman against cavalryman, the armor could deflect a slashing sword blow, and against infantry the breastplate was usually proof against a musket ball at 100 yds (90 m); but against a square of drilled infantrymen with fixed bayonets, firing three shots a minute and supported by artillery firing (roundshot, caseshot, and grape out to a range of 800 yds 730 m), which is what the French heavy cavalry faced at Waterloo in 1815, the armor turned these proud horsemen from battlewinners into vulnerable targets. Captain Cavalie Mercer of the British Royal Horse Artillery described his own battery's response to the French cavalry attacks in his memoir of the Waterloo campaign published in 1870:

I thus allowed them to advance unmolested until the head of the column might have been about fifty or sixty yards from us, and then gave the word, Fire! The effect was terrible. Nearly the whole leading rank fell at once; and the round-shot, penetrating the column, carried confusion throughout its extent. The ground, already encumbered with victims of the first struggle, became now almost impassable. Still, however, these devoted warriors struggled on, intent on reaching us. The thing was impossible. Our guns were served with astonishing activity, whilst the running fire of the two squares was maintained with spirit. Those who pushed forward over the heaps of carcasses of men and horses gained but a few paces in advance, there to fall in their turn and add to the difficulties of those succeeding them. The discharge of every gun was followed by a fall of men and horses like that of grass before a mower's scythe. When the horse alone was killed, we could see the cuirassiers divesting themselves of their encumbrances and making their escape on foot.

This is what armor had come to mean to professional soldiers like Mercer by 1815 – an "encumbrance". What of the centuries-old tradition of the armored horseman's superiority over the man on foot when he was stranded yards away from his enemy under murderous fire? Indeed, elsewhere on the field the Duke of Wellington – who, it has to be said, never had a very high regard for cavalry – referred to these unhorsed French as "turned turtles." Without his horse, the weight of armor actually put the man wearing it in danger, and, as Mercer witnessed, it was the very first thing to go in the run back through the lines.

Despite all the evidence that helmet and breastplate were now anachronisms in combat, these items of body armor still found favor with heavy cavalry regiments throughout Europe in the years after Waterloo and Napoleon's downfall.

The Prussians re-equipped entire regiments with discarded French breastplates in 1816, while in Britain in the early 1820s the newly crowned King George IV bedecked the Household Cavalry regiments with breastplates and high bearskin-crested helmets of the "Roman" type, which aped those of the French carabiniers.

There was more than an element of fashion statement about this use of armor in the early 19th century. The success of Napoleon's heavy horse had led to a wholesale copying of the French style of heavy cavalry uniform, in Britain for example. Between 1812 and 1814, the British dragoons and Household Cavalry had begun to be issued with a peaked helmet with high comb and black horsehair crest and "turban" very similar to that of the French cuirassiers.

The final withdrawal of breastplates and helmets from active service was to be, in some European countries, a very drawn-out business. The Prussians in their war with France in 1870-71 fielded regiments of cuirassiers with success, and withdrew the breastplate and steel helmet from front-line service only in 1889, after which they were retained for full dress and ceremonial use.

In contrast, one of the European military establishments most progressive in abandoning armor was that of Imperial Austria, which abolished its cavalry breastplate in 1860.

In Britain the Household Cavalry (the Blues and Life

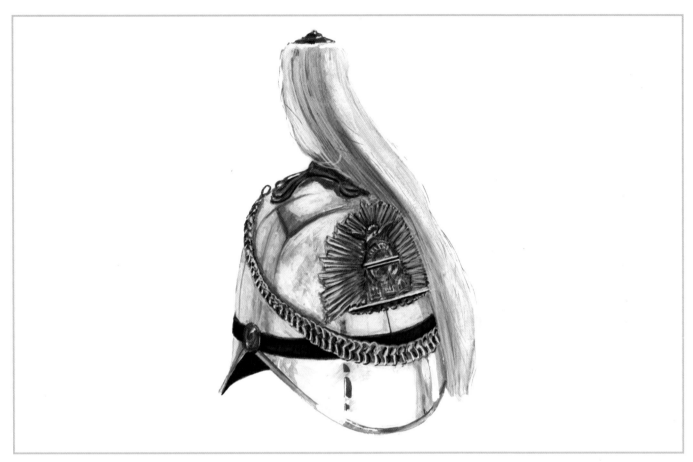

The British "Albert" pattern cavalry helmet c. 1850. This was the last pattern of metal cavalry helmet used in combat by the British in the 19th century, seeing service during the Crimean War of 1853-56. The plume was removed on active service.

Guards) continued the tradition of wearing helmet and breastplate, but since from 1815 to 1882 neither regiment saw combat service, the use of their armor became relegated to ceremonial wear.

In other British dragoon and heavy cavalry regiments varying styles of metal helmet were issued as service dress up to the beginning of the Crimean War in 1854. Based on Prussian and Russian designs, they were to prove hopelessly impractical under the rigorous campaign conditions the British Army were to face overseas.

An example of this was the experience of the 7th Dragoon Guards, who were posted to South Africa in 1845 and took part in the first war against the Boer settlers. Under an African sun, the dragoons fought at least one engagement wearing the 1834 pattern helmet of polished brass, complete with front and rear peaks and a high metal comb decorated with a lion's head.

Likewise the 6th Dragon Guards faced the mutineers in India in 1854 wearing the 1842 pattern 'Albert' helmet the same type that was to be taken to the Crimea. At least on active service the high plume was removed, the Dragoon Guards taking the extra precaution of wrapping a white linen cover – or puggaree – around the brass to offset what must have been the dreadful effects of the sun on a head encased in unventilated bare metal.

For the sake of the well-being of the troopers, this was a situation that could not be allowed to go on and, throughout the 1850s and 1860s, regimental commanders – those responsible in the British Army at this time for what their men wore in the field – came to conclude that in fighting campaigns overseas their men were better off without a helmet. Instead, on their own authority, lightweight tropical headgear was ordered and issued.

The 1842 Infantry Officers' pattern Prussian pickelhaube. This was the first helmet that was to see service with the Prussian and Imperial German armies until 1916. The 1842 pattern differs from the well-known design of 1914 in being far higher and carrying pronounced vizors both front and back.

The British tropical – or foreign service – helmet, of the type universally worn by both cavalry and infantry in all imperial campaigns up to the Second Boer War in 1899, owes its origins to this time of change. Its first pattern was introduced to all ranks during the Abyssinian campaign of 1868. This was military headgear, as defense not against the weapons of the enemy, but against the hazards of his climate. When the Household Cavalry finally rode back to war in Egypt in 1882, it was not their plumed polished helmets they were wearing, but canvas-covered cork foreign service helmets complete with smoked goggles and anti-fly face veils to combat the conditions in the desert.

The other piece of military headgear that epitomized the final decades of the 19th century, and the opening years of the 20th was the Prussian – later Imperial German – pickelhaube. Though not armor in its defined sense as a protection against a weapons blow – its leather construction precluded that – as a style and pattern it was to influence the design of German cavalry helmets as well as form the template for the famous German steel infantry helmet – the stahlhelm – of the following century's two world wars.

First approved for service in the Prussian military in October 1842, the pickelhaube continued a tradition among German-speaking nations of issuing the same pattern protective headgear to all branches and ranks of the army – a standard practice today, of course. It was first begun in the Austrian Empire in 1798 and copied by the Duchy of Württemburg in 1799 and the Kingdom of Bavaria in 1800.

Like these early types, the pickelhaube was made of heavy treated leather. The 1842 pattern sat very high on the head at 15 in (38 cm), unlike the close-fitting rounder models of later years, while its rear vizor extended out to provide protection for the neck. At no stage in its service history was the pickelhaube's famous spike designed to be an offensive weapon. It was purely decorative, being hollow and made of brass. In late models the spike was detachable, and was held on the crown of the helmet by a bayonet lug.

Although Imperial German infantry marched into Belgium in 1914 wearing the pickelhaube complete with its spike, by 1915 the German High Command, faced with the worsening conditions on the Western Front, had issued a directive that the spike should be removed when on service in the field.

Prussian artillery adopted the pickelhaube in 1844, and as a branch distinction the spike was replaced by a brass ball. Like the infantry pickelhaube the artillery pattern was phased out of service after the introduction of the first design of stahlhelm in 1916.

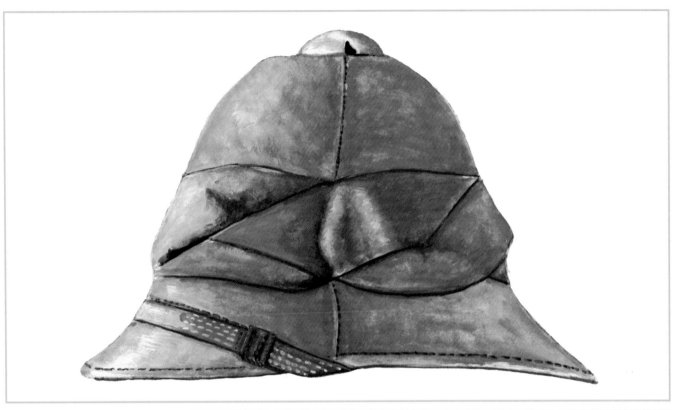

At the end of the 19th century the US Army also followed the British Army's lead in issuing tropical helmets. This example is a cork and khaki helmet from about 1900. It was worn on tropical service, particularly in the Philippines, and could be fitted with a brass spike and chin chain for ceremonial wear.

Imperial German Army tropical helmet of 1914. All colonial powers eventually adopted tropical headgear, and Imperial Germany was no exception. It was made of cork and khaki, and the metal base on the crown could take either a spike or a plume decoration.

A US Army vizored helmet of 1918. After the success of the French "Adrian" pattern helmet in 1916, all other combatant nations on the Western Front rushed to supply their own troops with "shrapnel" helmets. The perforated vizor was an innovation tried with many types of combat helmet before it was finally deemed impractical in the 1940s.

The First World War

As the 20th century began and Europe started her drift into the conflict that would become the First World War, an influential study was published in France in 1902 (and translated for the US War Department in 1906), comparing the infantry field equipment of the world's major armies.

It provides a perfect glimpse into the orthodox military thinking in those pre-war days and reveals that the personal protection of the infantry soldier against shot and shell simply wasn't an issue of the time. It also reveals that the military establishments of the world's major powers had no idea what they were about to inflict on one another just twelve years later.

The mobility of the infantryman was the study's major point of reference, and any additional weight added to his average personal load of 60-lb (27-kg) pack and 10-lb (4.5-kg) rifle – the standard weight carried by the infantry since the Napoleonic Wars – was deemed unacceptable. The British foreign service helmet was judged to be the finest campaign helmet of the time because its cork construction was light and "lightness should be the first quality of the headdress of the foot soldier." Even the German pickelhaube was considered too heavy to be truly practical for the infantryman on the march, and metal headgear was dismissed out of hand, as "The employment of metal would make too heavy a helmet, one insupportable to the foot soldier."

Infantry in Europe and North America had not worn protective armor of any description for over 250 years. Theirs was a branch of the service that had evolved by the end of the 19th century to be the dominant force on the battlefield, and it had achieved this by the use of arms, unit discipline, and the unflinching courage of the individual soldier in the face of enemy fire. The very idea that the foot soldier would seek out and wear protective armor as a personal defense was a notion as ludicrous as it was insulting.

There did exist a precedent for wearing armor, but it was restricted to conditions of siege warfare, where men took post for long periods under the direct fire of the enemy and could neither advance or retreat. Such conditions were historically suffered mostly by engineers, miners, or laborers digging earthworks, and were not ones that respectable infantrymen would wish on themselves for any length of time.

There had been some minor developments in armored protection in the 1890s. In 1894 a Captain Boynton of the British Army designed and trialed a steel rifle shield. Weighing 6 lbs (2.7 kg), the shield was unique in that it was fitted directly onto the rifle, being hinged under the barrel so that it gave protection to the soldier while he was either standing or firing prone.

The Japanese also took an interest in armored shields, developing a small individual pattern, which they used in some numbers during the Russo-Japanese War of 1904-05. Weighing 18 lbs (8 kg) and measuring 12 x 19 in (30 x 47 cm) in size, this steel shield is important in that it had a backing of leather stuffed with hair. This acted to absorb the metal splinters produced by a bullet strike, the Japanese being among the first to realize that the splinters could be as lethal as the bullet itself.

Developments had also occurred in body armor. In 1897 a Russian, Casimir Zeglin, had introduced a bullet-resistant waistcoat to the public in a series of trials in New York. Made of silk, the Zeglin was the first piece of soft armor to be purpose-made in the West in centuries.

Zeglin's material was later used to cover and line a metal vest designed in Russia and used in numbers by Russian officers in the war with Japan. Made of chrome-nickel plate, the vest covered only the front of the body but could resist a rifle bullet at 2,300 ft/sec (700m/sec) fired from 200 yds (182 m).

Elsewhere, commercial manufacturers were taking an interest in metal body armor, and between 1899 and 1901 in Europe and North America the "Rome" breastplate, the "Payot" cuirass and the

Prior to the First World War, the only type of body armor used in combat was that employed in sieges. This vest of closely linked steel plates was used in France during the siege of Paris in 1870. Body armors of iron plate are also known to have been used by the Union Army during the siege of Petersburg, Virginia, in 1864.

"Benedetti" body shield were all patented, trialed, or put on the open market. Even military writers, particularly those in France, were coming to the conclusion that against modern weapons such as the machine-gun some form of man-portable defense was going to be necessary.

For all its killing power, it was not to be the machine-gun that brought armor back to service in the coming war world, but the widespread use of high-explosive ordnance.

The outbreak of the First World War in August 1914 and its degeneration on the Western Front to static trench warfare by December created tactical problems that no one could have foreseen. Foremost among these was how to attack an enemy who rarely showed himself above the parapet of his trench. An answer was becoming clear to all sides by early 1915: pour explosive ordnance on him from above.

Artillery shells, mortar bombs, and grenades became the offensive weapons of this new kind of warfare, and the men

A 19th-century engineer's siege helmet. From the 1700s to 1916 these were the only types of metal combat helmet used by foot soldiers in European armies. From the design it is clear it is for the use of a man in a static position under fire and would be of little use to a soldier on the move, as it cuts out all lateral vision and would even prevent the wearer hearing orders.

standing in the trenches wearing only caps, kepis, or pickelhaubes began to suffer heavily from the rain of exploding steel. By 1915 it is believed that up to 80 percent of all wounds treated by British, French, and German Army surgeons were being caused by metal splinters ("shrapnel") from ordnance, travelling more slowly than bullets, at middle or low velocity; the French doctors came to the conclusion that among their men 1 in 4 such wounds was proving fatal.

One of the first people to attempt some defense against this danger was General Adrian of the French Army. In December 1914 Adrian had been issuing steel skull caps to his men to test their efficiency under fire. Little more than a metal lining to the standard issue kepi, the skull cap, though only .197 in (5mm) thick and weighing 9 oz (252 g), was able to resist up to 60 percent of shrapnel hits.

Encouraged by these results and driven by the pressing need to reduce casualty levels, the French Government put the skull cap into large-scale production. By March 1915, 700,000 had been manufactured and sent to the trenches. While this stop-gap measure was underway, the French Army's "Adrian" pattern steel helmet completed its design and also went into production.

Made of pressed mild steel barely 4/100 in (1mm) thick, from dies originally designed to produce firemen's helmets, the "Adrian" was the first combat helmet of the modern era to see front-line service, the first examples reaching the trenches in July 1915.

The "Adrian" came in three sizes and of all the helmets subsequently designed during the war was the most complicated to manufacture. Seventy separate processes pressed and assembled its three major sections: dome, crest, and brim (which came in two pieces, front and back). Nevertheless, the initial production run was over a million, and by fall 1917 two manufacturers alone were turning out 7,500 finished helmets a day from 200 presses.

The arrival of the French Army's helmet in the frontline quickly encouraged the British and Germans to develop their own armored headgear.

The French "Adrian" pattern helmet of 1916. As first issued, the helmets were painted blue, and a branch of service badge was attached to the front.

The British Mk I "Brodie" pattern helmet. This was the pattern adopted by the US War Department on America's entry into the First World War and designated the M1917. The first units of the AEF to arrive on the Western Front in 1917 are known to have worn the French "Adrian" pattern during their first weeks in the trenches.

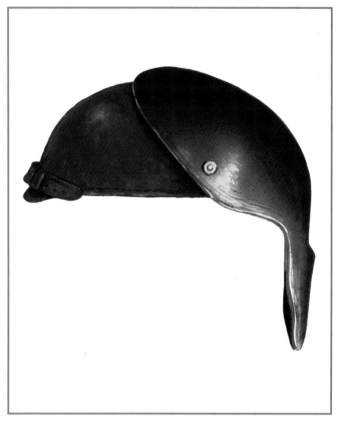

Right: The German "Gaede" trench helmet of 1915, the first kind of metal combat helmet to replace the obsolete pickelhaube. Like many types of armor in the modern era, the "Gaede" owed its development to the pressing needs of the men under fire in the front line.

Far right: The Model 1916 German helmet, the stahlhelm. The two large lugs found on the front of this pattern supported the separate brow armor, which was meant to provide ballistic protection to the front of the head. Though a good idea, the brow armor unbalanced the helmet and was unpopular with the men.

The British Mk I "Brodie" pattern (see page 115 for illustration) was designed in mid-1915 by John Brodie of London. It was in the shape of a shallow dome with a broad brim, which followed that of the "chapel de fer" helmet of the 14th century. Though Brodie acknowledged the antecedents, the choice of shape had more to do with its ease of manufacture: the helmet could be stamped out of a piece of sheet steel in a single operation.

Particular care was given to the helmet's inner lining, which in the Second World War would be refered to as its "suspension system." The object was to keep the wearer's head away from the bare metal, provide equal distribution of the weight, and create sufficient ventilation. The lining was also to provide an element of protection against the indentation and penetration of the outer steel shell.

Brodie, typical of the new generation of armorers, was heavily influenced by scientific and medical analysis of the types of threat posed to the helmet and its wearer. It was realised that a blow powerful enough to create a serious indentation to the outer shell could cause lethal injury to the head – the condition known to armor designers later in the century as "blunt trauma."

To gauge the effectiveness of the design, ballistic tests were carried out – a typical example being the firing of a shrapnel ball at the helmet at an average velocity of 700 ft/sec (213m/sec). As the need to bring the helmet to production was so great, such tests were designed only to prove the minimum level of protection the helmet could offer. To put this into context, the velocity of the .311 nickel-steel round from the German's Mauser rifle was 2,093 ft/sec (638m/sec).

Although the Mk I "Brodie" was never promoted as being bullet-proof, it did provide some protection to head and shoulders from low velocity shrapnel from above, and at 1 lb 11 oz (756 g) was light enough to wear for quite long periods. Its one major failing was that it provided no protection at all to the face or throat.

The Mk I began reaching British trenches in November 1915, at first in very small numbers – 50

Another criticism of the Model 1916 was that coverage over the ears made it difficult for the soldier to hear. This problem was tackled with the final German helmet pattern of the First World War, the Model 1918, which featured distinctive cutaways around both ears.

helmets per battalion of 500 men was not unusual — and was issued only to posted sentries and specialist grenade-throwers or "bombers" in the front line.

The response of the soldiers to this reappearance of what to them was a piece of medieval gear was mixed. Many did not even know what to call it. Captain J.C. Dunn of the Royal Welsh Fusiliers reported in his journal for March 1916:

March 9th — Steel helmets issued. Many did not know them by any other name than "tin hat." "Battle-bowler" strove for a few days for recognition. When we wore cloth caps I never knew a man seek to shield his head from flying metal although he were bare-headed, but when we wore tin-hats and metal was flying about I never knew of a bare-headed man who did not bolt for cover; even in a deep dug-out there were few who did not reach for their helmet if shells burst outside.

On the other side of No-Man's Land, by 1915 the German High Command had accepted the fact that the pickelhaube was now obsolete, but had been slow in commissioning a replacement. This had proved unpopular with some front-line German units who, tired of the wait, began to improvise their own

protective headgear.

In the Vosges mountains of central France, Battlegroup Gaede was one of these. Under the authority of its lieutenant-colonel, a trench helmet was designed and manufactured, consisting of a steel plate secured onto a leather skull cap lined with cloth. The circular plate was roughly .234 in (6 mm) thick and covered only the front part of the skull, though it did extend down across the forehead to form a noseguard. The "Gaede" helmet weighed approximately 4.5 lbs (2 kg) and saw service for barely a year before it was replaced by Germany's new standard pattern steel combat helmet.

The stahlhelm, M1916, like the French "Adrian" helmet, began its development outside the auspices of the military's high command. Two men were primarily responsible: Friedrich Schwerd, a professor of engineering, and Dr August Bier, consulting surgeon to the XVIII Corps. Their combined recommendations for a one-piece shrapnel helmet reached the Imperial General Staff in Berlin in August 1915, and by September specifications had been draw up and initial

Right: The British "EOB" body armor of 1917. It is worn with the high silk ballistic collar, which was meant to protect the wearer from shell splinters traveling horizontally. The collar highlighted the main failure of the "Brodie" design.

Far right: One of the experimental forms of armor developed in the United States in 1918; this is the "Brewster" sentinel armor. Though providing complete protection for the soldier, it prevents him from doing anything other than just standing.

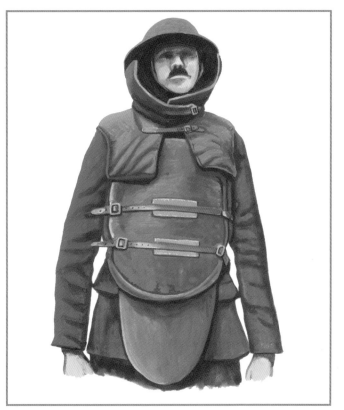

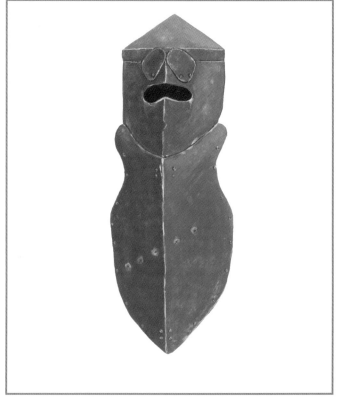

orders placed.

The helmet underwent field trials with an assault battalion in December and went into large-scale production in January 1916. Chief of the General Staff, General Falkenhayn, authorized its introduction to the German Field Army on the Western Front the following month.

Officially designated Stahlschutzhelm (steel protective helmet) Model 1916, the helmet was stamped from a single sheet of chromium-nickel steel. It came in six sizes. The pronounced rim projecting from the crown provided the best protection of any helmet in service during the war. The serious drawback to the M1916 was that the steel was only .0429 in (1.1 mm) thick.

The reason for this was the steel shortage brought on by Britain's naval blockade, though some official rationalizations were put forward, such as the idea that the helmet was designed to be light enough to be worn at all times and the fact that a fully effective armored helmet would weigh at least 13 lbs (6 kg).

To provide sentries with some protection against small arms fire, the stahlhelm (illustrated on page 116) was designed to be used with a steel plate 0.195 in (5mm) thick (known as a "brow armor") which slotted onto two lugs at the front of the helmet, which doubled as ventilation holes. Though 5 percent of all stahlhelms were supposed to be issued with this frontal plate, steel shortages prevented this figure from ever being reached. The plate was in any case unpopular with the troops (reports in 1917 had them being used to strengthen trenches) and production had ceased by January 1918.

Later that year a second pattern stahlhelm made its appearance in response to criticism from the front line that the M1916 shape covered the ears, blocking the sound of incoming shells. The M1918 followed the same stahlhelm pattern but provided cutaway areas over both ears. The M1918 saw only limited service before the Armistice in November.

Both models of stahlhelm were designed with a variant that featured a face vizor for the face and eyes. The protection of these vital areas was of great concern to all sides and a lot of work was undertaken,

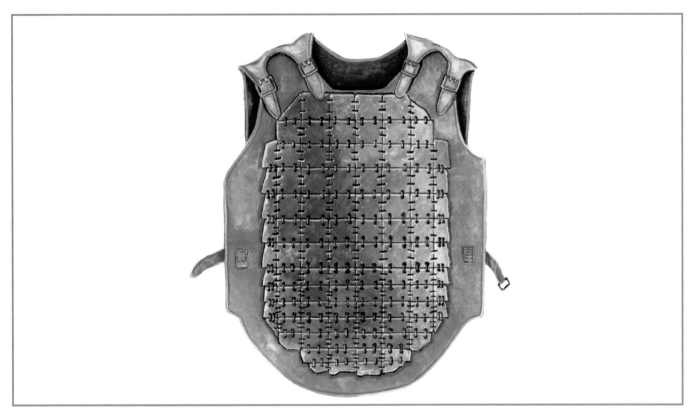

The "Franco-British cuirass" of 1916. This early type of trench armor uses bare metal on a material backing. Later experience would show that the armor plates needed a sturdy cloth covering to provide camouflage, and prevent splinters and bullets from ricocheting or disintegrating, which could cause horrific injury.

particuarly by the British, to produce an effective armor defense. In 1915 one of the first to be proposed to the British Army was the "Berkeley" face shield. It consisted simply of a steel plate pierced by vertical and transverse slits for eyes and nose, which fitted up under the service cap.

The eye defense that saw the widest use was a chain-mail face veil devised by Captain Cruise of the Royal Army Medical Corps and introduced in 1916. The veil was made of closely woven steel links and was secured to the brim of the Mk I helmet and under the nose of the wearer by chain links to the helmet's chin strap. Other types of experimental eye protection included various types of anti-splinter goggles made of metal or leather.

The French and Belgian armies, as well as the US Army, on its arrival on the Western Front in 1917, all experimented with face vizors to their helmets. However, protecting the face always created two serious practical drawbacks: the soldier's vision was impaired, and aiming a rifle became almost impossible. What is more, the advent of gas warfare in 1915 and the need to don the new gas respirators quickly and efficiently made any kind of face armor a hazard.

The soldiers who did benefit directly from face protection were the crews of the new British tanks. The armor plate on the inside of the tank was prone to splinter when hit, injuring the men inside, and in response tank crews by 1918 were wearing a leather half-mask over their eyes with a "Cruise" chain veil covering the mouth and nose.

The combat helmet in all its various styles had proven a success on the Western Front in 1916, and its use soon spread to other armies and theaters of the war. The following year the Belgians, Italians, Serbs, and Russians had all adopted the French "Adrian", while the US War Department opted for a revised pattern of the British Mk I "Brodie", designated the M1917.

In contrast to this rapid re-introduction of the armored helmet, widespread use of body armor during the First World War did not occur. It was of course a logical step to extend armor protection from the soldier's head to the rest of his body, but achieving

Right: A British tank crewman's splinter goggles and chain face veil of 1918. Though vizors proved impractical to soldiers in the trenches, they were useful to tank crews; the armor plate on the first tanks was pliable enough to produce dangerous splinters on the inside when struck

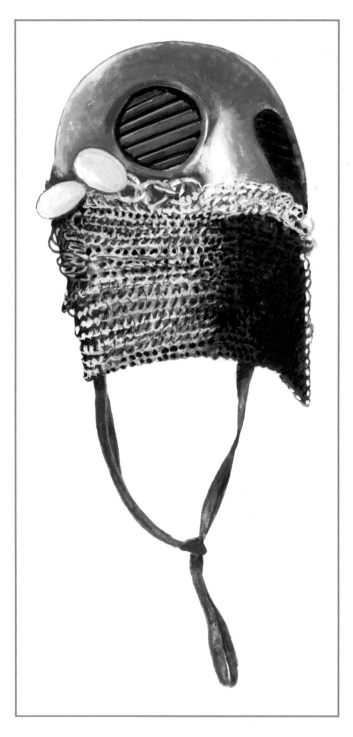

Top far right: Though vizors on combat helmets were never widely employed, some form of eye protection was considered vital. Various kinds of splinter goggle were developed in Britain and France and were usually made of leather and metal, as with this British example of 1917.

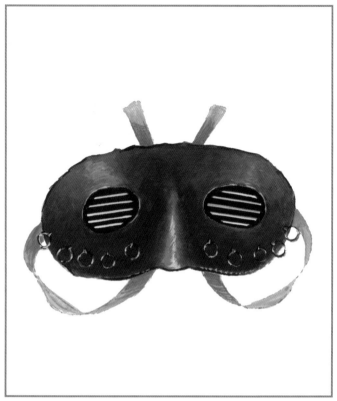

Right: The most widely produced eye protector developed in the First World War was the British "Cruise" chain-link face veil. Though cheap and simple to attach to the brim of the "Brodie" helmet, it nevertheless still seriously restricted the vision of the soldier.

The French answer to the problem of eye protection was the shrapnel vizor on the "Adrian" pattern helmet.

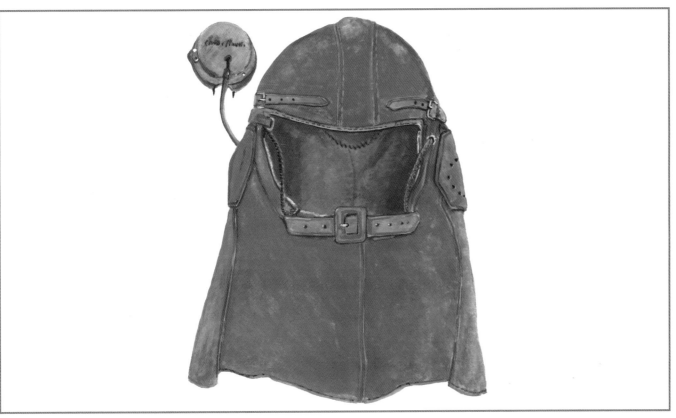

Leather flying helmet used by air gunners of the British Army's Royal Flying Corps in 1915. Steel combat helmets for aviators were not successfully introduced until the USAAF's developments of 1942-43. During the First World War both British and French helmets were impractical in the open cockpits of the time, though the stahlhelm Model 1916 was successfully worn by German flyers for ground-attack missions.

The British "Drayfield" armor system of 1918. The flat metal plates would certainly provide protection from blast and shell fragments, but would be of little use against a direct strike from a rifle bullet.

this in practical terms meant solving a series of problems that armorers had never had to face before.

The supersonic velocity of modern small arms ammunition meant that an armor had not only to stop the bullet but also to absorb the impact of the blow, not only to prevent injury to the wearer, but also to prevent the bullet breaking up on impact into lethal splinters. There was also the problem of weight. The metal of the armor had to be heavy enough to resist a strike, but light enough for a soldier to wear it and fight.

In Britain, some of the commercially manufactured body armors that were appearing by 1915 showed a high degree of sophistication in trying to counter the threat of a bullet impact. The "Portobank Bodyshield" for example consisted of five separate layers: a khaki-covered felt fronting a steel plate, which was then backed by surgical wadding and an inner cotton lining.

Some British armors such as the "Chemico" and the "Drayfield" of 1916 featured groin plates for greater protection, while further experiments into soft armor led to the development of a high ballistic collar made of silk. This stood proud of the shoulders and was designed to compensate for the Mk I helmet's lack of neck protection.

Most British armors took trench conditions into account and were covered with a camouflage of khaki drill. This not only protected the armor from rust, it also deadened any sound the metal might make - an important point in trench warfare.

If the British had grasped one of the fundamentals of modern body armor design – that it should be as inconspicuous as possible – others who developed body armor during the war did not.

The German Infantrie Panzer armor, introduced in 1917 and issued two per infantry company, consisted of an unpadded breastplate and four jointed groin plates – the plates being up to .14 in (3.5 mm) thick. The armor came in two sizes weighing 20 lbs (9 kg) and 24 lbs (11 kg). There was no back plate.

The weight made it too heavy to move effectively, and its shape restricted the use of a rifle or the throwing of grenades. Nevertheless, the Infantrie Panzer proved useful to sentries and those fighting from fixed positions such as machine-gun posts.

Other combatant nations who developed body

armor during these latter years of war included France and Italy, the Italians taking a special interest and issuing armors and helmets of steel plate to special raiding units known as Arditti.

The country that undertook the greatest level of research and development into armor after 1917 was the United States. Faced with entry into a war that had already cost the lives of millions and to which no one could see an end before 1919, the United States began a crash program.

Undeterred by the fact that as a nation it had no experience or history of armor design or construction, it nevertheless raided every domestic source of information – including exhibits from the Metropolitan Museum of Art in New York – and by 1918 had produced prototypes of armors ranging from a three-piece full basinet helmet for machine-gun crews to a lightweight plate armor for the proposed offensives of 1919.

None of these armors ever reached beyond the prototype stage – Germany's defeat of 1918 brought the program to a close. This work in the United States did, however, clarify thinking as to armor's future role in warfare.

After the experience on the Western Front all military authorities agreed that some form of armor protection, especially for the head, had returned to stay. As regards body armor, though, conclusions were mixed. The need for its use in certain circumstances was obvious, but technologically armor still meant steel plate, which created the old difficulties of weight against combat effectiveness. It would be another 40 years and another world war before these problems would begin to find a solution.

The most extreme form of body armor protection was this prototype mini-tank developed in Britain in 1917. How the man inside was meant to propel this monster over shell-torn ground perhaps only the designer could answer!

Right: The British "Portobank" body shield. This design features elements later used in armored vests of the 1980s, namely a ballistic front plate surrounded by a padded vest, which also served to carry items of equipment.

Far right: The far cruder German Infantrie-Panzer of 1918. The first versions of the Infantrie-Panzer did not even feature a padded backing as a defense against impact trauma. There was no back plate to this armor.

Far left:
An Italian body shield of 1917. After coming into the war on the Allied side in 1915, the Italians took a keen interest in developing body armor, and first issued plate armor to their special "Arditti" raiding units in 1916. This is a later pattern of armor, which doubles as a rifle shield. The two metal "legs" that support it on the ground can be seen folded away on either side of the soldier's chest.

Left: A prototype light infantry armor and helmet developed in the US in 1918 for the proposed AEF offensives of 1919. Though the war ended before this armor could be trialed, the helmet, known as the Model 5A, later influenced the design of the famous US M1 combat helmet of 1941.

The Soviet pattern 1936 combat helmet. Design influences of both the German stahlhelm and the French "Adrian" can be seen. It was clear by the 1930s that the 'pot' shape would be the optimum design for future combat helmets.

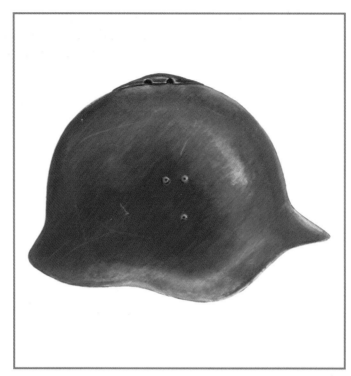

Between the Wars

The inter-war years of the 1920s and '30s, though ostensibly years of peace, saw a growth in the use of body armor by civilians. Gangsterism and political violence were widespread in many countries, and in supplying a ready-to-wear means of personal protection, body armor made the easy transition from the battlefield to the city street.

Among the most successful armors of the time was the "Wisbrod" vest made in the United States in the 1930s. Consisting of overlapping steel plates encased in a rubberized plastic, the "Wisbrod" could withstand a .45 round from a Thompson sub-machine gun. Its inventor, Eliot Wisbrod, went to extreme lengths to promote his vest, undergoing thousands of live-fire demonstrations with his vest, using himself as the target. His demonstrations paid off, and police departments in Los Angeles, Boston, and Chicago became customers, as did some notable politicians such as Franklin D. Roosevelt and Josef Stalin.

Military involvement in armor development ceased almost entirely around the world in the 1920s, and it was not until the drive to rearm by the militarists in Germany, Italy, and Japan in the mid-1930s that the process began again in earnest.

Japan was one of the first, introducing a "pot" style of steel helmet in 1932, a move followed a year later by the Italians with their Model 933. Two years after that the new Nazi regime in Germany put the Model 1935 stahlhelm into production to coincide with the reintroduction of conscription.

Smaller and lighter than the M1916, the M1935 came in five sizes weighing from 29 oz to 42 oz (0.82 kg - 1.2 kg). It featured a new design of adjustable suspension on the inside and a distinctive crimping of the metal round the rim. The crimping was discontinued as an economy measure in 1943.

Elsewhere, the Soviet Union, concerned to protect its revolution also invested militarily, introducing new patterns of helmet in 1928 and 1936. Both patterns featured a small crest protecting a ventilation hole in the crown. At the onset of war with Germany in 1941, the Soviets adopted a helmet closely resembling the Italian M933: broad, pot-shaped, and sufficiently low at the sides and back to cover the ears and lower head.

This pattern would see service with the Soviet armed forces until the early 1990s.

Other countries in Europe, seeing the growing military threat posed by Germany and its Italian ally also began to look to their defense, and from 1934 Czechoslovakia, Poland, and the Netherlands all adopted steel helmets based on the pot shape.

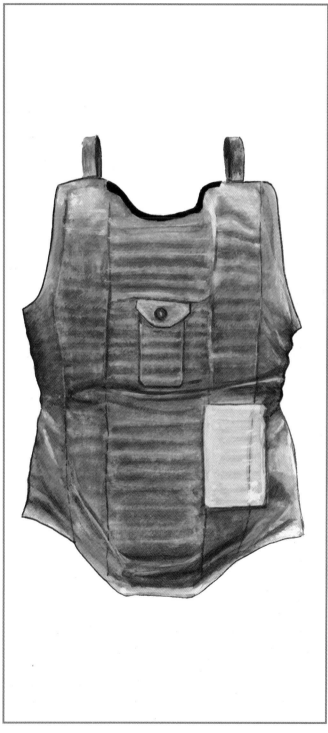

Far left:
The Soviet pattern 1941. This is the type of helmet worn by the Red Army during the Second World War, and saw action from the gates of Moscow to the Chancellery in Berlin. Ironically it is actually based on the Italian 933 design introduced by Mussolini's fascists in 1933.

Left:
A pattern of Japanese body armor, c. 1930s, made of linked overlapping steel plates in a canvas vest. Contrary to the tradition of the suicide charge, the Japanese are reported to have developed three different patterns of body armor during the Second World War.

The first pattern German fallschirmjäger helmet of 1936. A camouflage cover for the helmet was introduced in 1941.

The Second World War

The only major countries to ignore this worldwide trend to modernize and upgrade the combat helmet were the democracies of Britain, France, and the United States. Apparently helmets designed in 1915 were thought sufficient to fight any future war, and the Mk II "Brodie," the "Adrian" and the M1917 were all still standard issue when the Second World War broke out.

Germany's defeat of France in 1940 finished the use of the "Adrian" as a service helmet, while Britain's retreat from the continent and her months fighting alone from June 1940 to January 1942 delayed the production of a new design of infantry helmet, the Mk III, until late 1943.

The Mk III's broad 'turtle back' design provided better balance and an overall increase in protection of over 10 percent. Though at 2 lbs 9 oz (1.1 kg), 4 oz (112 g) heavier than the Mk II, it proved popular with the troops. Unfortunately its availability was limited, and was issued only to the British and Canadian assault regiments by the time of the D-Day landings in June, 1944. It never completely replaced the Mk II until after the war.

Only the United States had the manufacturing capacity, the money, and the time to develop a new combat helmet before she, too, had to fight, and even then the decision was left almost too late.

Throughout the 1930s, the M1917 had been criticized for its poor balance and lack of overall protection. It was also criticized for not being an American design. The War Department research in 1918 had shown that the "pot" was the optimum shape for a helmet – providing good overall balance with superior levels of protection especially from horizontal blows. But it was not until August 1940 that these findings were at last acted upon.

With Hitler triumphant in Europe, and America's entry into war an ever-stronger possibility, action was finally taken. The War Department refused to sign a contract for another 2 million M1917s and asked for new designs to be submitted. The result was to be the M1 helmet, that most potent symbol of the US at war and the most widely used piece of armor in history.

Unique among combat helmets to that time, the M1 consisted of two separate pieces: an outer steel shell, into which fitted a lightweight inner liner, onto which the chinstrap and suspension system were attached. The complete helmet weighed 2 lbs 15 oz (1.3 kg). The steel shell was ballistically tested to withstand a .45 caliber round at 800ft/sec (244 m/sec), a 200 ft/sec (61 m/sec) improvement on the M1917, and was approved for service on June 9, 1941.

The shell was straightforward to produce, although it took 27 separate processes, but finding a durable liner proved more difficult. The first pattern was a complicated affair made of processed fiber covered in cotton twill and trimmed with leather. Prone to fray and easily damaged by water, this was declared unfit for service in 1941 and replaced with a more successful pattern made from plastic-impregnated cotton.

Production of the steel shells was concentrated at McCord Radiator and Manufacturing Corp. in Detroit, which by 1945 could turn out one helmet shell every 22 minutes. Production of the liners was divided between 10 companies operating out of Illinois, Massachusetts, Michigan, Ohio, and Pennsylvania. By the end of the Second World War these companies had produced between them 22 million steel shells and over 33 million inner liners.

Variants of the M1 produced during the war included the Mk 2 US Navy "talkers" helmet. Developed in 1942, this outsized piece of headgear featured a fixed waterproofed insert of foam rubber and was designed specifically to be worn over radio headphones.

There was also the M2 airborne helmet for paratroops and glider-borne infantry. Using the same steel shell as the M1, it differed only in the extra padding in the inner liner and in a more secure and supportive system of chinstrap, which featured a chin cup.

The Model 1935 German stahlhelm. This is the 1943 pattern, which for purposes of economy differed from the original 1935 version in not having the distinctive crimping round the rim and in not featuring national and branch of service decals on either side.

The Mk III British combat helmet. The Mk I of the First World War was replaced in 1936 by the Mk II, though this differed only in the design of its suspension liner and chinstrap. The Mk III was a completely new design, but did not see full-scale production and service in the British Army until after the Second World War.

HELMET COVERS

One of the main drawbacks to the use of steel for combat helmets was that as a material it was so difficult to camouflage. The very properties that had characterized the steel armors of earlier centuries and made them so attractive – shining reflective surface and hard distinctive profile – could in modern warfare betray the position of a soldier and bring down enemy fire. Very quickly after the reintroduction of steel helmets in 1916 it was realized that to prevent their carers from becoming targets the helmets were going to have to be camouflaged and made as indistinct as possible.

The simplest method was to paint the helmet a neutral color. This proved insufficient and was improved on by the Germans who by July 1918 had begun painting the M1916 in a three-color disruptive pattern, said to camouflage the helmet up to 65 yd (60 m).

Plain paint failed to reduce the glare from the helmet in direct sun or moonlight, and to reduce this various solutions were tried during the two world wars. Mixing the paint with sand was popular. The Germans also tried paint and wool dust during the First World War, while the Americans tried paint and ground cork on the first M1s in 1941. The British and Canadians found a solution during the Second World War by covering their helmets with green string netting, a method followed in 1944 by both the US and German armies.

The netting could also secure foliage or hessian "scrim" to the helmet. The Germans' method of securing camouflage to the M1935 was by a system of straps around the crown. Before 1939 this was an issue item made of leather and secured by metal clips and a buckle. Later in the war the men had to improvise, and tyre inner tubes and even chicken wire were put to use.

By far the most efficient and simplest method of camouflaging a helmet was to give it a cloth cover. During the First World War both the French and the Germans had covers specifically designed for their helmets, while the British and Empire troops had to make do with improvised hessian covers made from sand bags – a method also used by some British infantry units in 1939-40.

It was Hitler's Waffen-SS that first used helmet covers in camouflage pattern material, during the invasion of France in 1940, a move followed a year later by the Luftwaffe's fallschirmjäger paratroopers and the Army. In the United States camouflage pattern covers for the M1 were rejected by the Army, but adopted by the Marine Corps, which developed three patterns of reversible cover during their Pacific campaign of 1942-45. The US Department of Defense extended the use of helmet covers to the Army in 1963, and they were ubiquitous among US ground forces during the Vietnam War of 1965-73.

Unlike the US M2, the helmets produced for the German and British airborne troops were not adaptations of existing infantry designs, but were specifically developed to act as both combat and crash helmets.

The German fallschirmjäger helmet was introduced in 1936 for the use of the Luftwaffe's first airborne units founded the same year. Visually striking, the helmet looked like a rimless M1935 stahlhelm, but included the typical features of an airborne helmet such as extra interior padding and a stronger chinstrap to secure the helmet at both the front and rear.

The British airborne helmet was first introduced in 1940 and, like the American M2, was used by both paratroopers and glider-borne infantry. The steel shell was round, so it did not provide the same degree of ballistic protection as either the British Mk III or the US M1. The same shell was also used by the Royal Armored Corps and British Army motorcycle despatch riders after 1943.

In contrast to this growing sophistication and specialization in some areas of helmet design, elsewhere there were still some armorers who retained a belief in the usefulness of metal face vizors. In Germany a patent was taken out in 1938 for a hinged-perforated vizor attachment to the M1935 stahlhelm, while in the United States drawings exist for a movable vizor for the M1. Neither of these proposals even reached the prototype stage.

In Britain it was another matter. Examples of the "Cruise" vizor for the Mk II helmet were manufactured and trialed in 1940 with the British Expeditionary Force in France. Practical, insofar as it could be clipped up out of the way under the rim of the helmet, the "Cruise" was on the verge of large-scale field trials when the retreat from Dunkirk left 5,000 vizors sitting in England without an army for them to go to. Undeterred, advocates of the vizor had it trialed in Britain through the fall of 1940. Results finally concluded that it was impossible to see through in rain or poor light, and it was quietly dropped in 1941.

The adherence by some in Britain to this kind of First World War thinking on armor protection also led to the development of a lightweight steel body armor. Trialed in early 1941, the armor could be described as being more of a set than a suit, comprising as it did just three individually shaped .039 in (1mm) thick steel plates, linked by webbing straps. Two plates lay on the front of the body covering the heart and belly, and a third (an inverted "T" shape) covered the lower back and spine. The plates were curved for a close fit, backed with felt and covered in canvas. The whole set weighed 3.5 lbs (1.5 kg).

Despite complete indifference to it from commanders in the field, the armor won government approval in 1942, and plans were made to manufacture sets for every combat soldier in the British Army. As it was, production ceased in 1944 with only 200,000 completed, of which only 15,000 were ever issued to the troops, most going to men of the Airborne divisions in preparation for the invasion of Europe. Though produced for the safety and welfare of the soldiers, the armor was never popular with the rank and file, who saw it as just another encumbrance. None of the sets was ever used in action.

The British Army may have been hostile to the armor, but the RAF certainly was not. Seeing a use

The US M2 airborne helmet. A variant of the M1, the M2 featured a sturdier suspension liner and a four-point strap with a leather chin cup. The leather cup was replaced by webbing straps in 1944.

The 1941 US M1 helmet. In this example the inner liner is secured to the outer steel shell by means of its chinstrap over the front brim. The use of netting was an attempt to cut down on glare from the steel and was adopted from a British idea. The US Army used the British/Canadian pattern during the D-Day landing, receiving their own pattern of netting in December.

The ringkraken (gorget) of the German Army 1945. Worn by the feldjäger-kommando security police behind the front line, this gorget was not a decorative throwback but symbolized the power over life or death.

The feldjäger-kommando was formed in late 1944 to stiffen the resolve of those defending the Third Reich by any means necessary, which meant, in effect, "flying courts-martial," summary executions, and even the wholesale impressment of second echelon troops into combat units.

GORGET

As a symbol of rank and duty the history of the gorget goes back to the 17th century. A last vestige of medieval plate armor, this metal neck plate was retained by European armies throughout the 18th century as a distinguishing mark of the "officer and gentleman."

It was worn by officers of the British Army from 1660 to 1830, abolished in France after the 1789 revolution, and even features in American military history. Worn by colonial officers during the French and Indian Wars of the 1760s — there is an early portrait of George Washington wearing one c. 1772 — it was seen again on some officers of the Continental Army during the War of Independence, though it was abolished soon afterwards.

In Germany the gorget - or ringkragen — enjoyed its longest period of use. Falling out of favor early in the 19th century, the gorget was readopted by some senior cavalry regiments of the Imperial German Army, beginning with the 2nd (Pomeranian) Cuirassiers in 1895. It was scrapped after the fall of Kaiser Wilhelm II in 1918, but made a return in 1933 as part of Adolf Hitler's remilitarization.

Always keen to exploit traditional symbols of power and authority, the Nazis reintroduced the gorget for use in the armed services and the party security organizations, the SS and SA. Worn by color or standard bearers and by honor guards, the gorget was also a duty sign of military police units, and as such gave these unloved members of the second echelon their common nickname "chained dogs" among the lower ranks.

for the armor, the air force issued 65,000 sets to its flight crews.

Body armor for flyers was not a new idea. From the early years of combat aviation in the First World War, air services around the world had seen the sense in trying to protect crewmen from anti-aircraft fire. The Russians were the first to introduce armor for aviators, kitting out some of their bomber crews in

1915. This early experiment failed because the armor was too heavy and restricted the size of the aircraft's bomb load.

As aviation technology improved, allowing heavier loads to be carried, by 1917 both the French and the Germans were working on types of armor protection for their airmen. The French developed a prototype frontal plate, jointed at the groin and with a pronounced lip at the top of the chest to protect the head and throat from strikes from below. At about the same time some German airmen, particularly those flying ground attack sorties, began to replace their leather flying helmets with the M1916 stahlhelm. In the United States the armor development program of 1918 also included work on a close-fitting, lightweight steel aviator's helmet, though the war had finished before it could be trialed.

The interior of the third pattern British Airborne helmet, 1944. The adjustable suspension liner is typical of the systems originally developed in the First World War. This helmet, however, is designed for airborne operations and has additional padding in the crown and a heavily padded rim.

Front and rear views of the British "MRC" (Medical Research Council) armor developed in 1942. Despite government proposals that all British Army combat troops be issued with this armor, only 15,000 sets were issued to combat units, and none was ever taken into action.

America's entry into the Second World War in 1941 would see a rebirth of interest in armor for aircrew, and would focus on the bomber squadrons of the US Army's Eighth Air Force flying missions into Nazi-occupied Europe from eastern England.

Daylight precision bombing was the chosen strategy of this offensive, and the US Army Air Force (USAAF) stuck to it with an absolute conviction in its war-winning potential. At the beginning of operations in August 1942, however, little thought was given to the protection of the air crews. It was thought perhaps that their B-17s and -24s would be flying high enough to be out of harm's way. Within two months this assumption was shown to be wildly optimistic; crews were taking heavy casualties from anti-aircraft fire.

Medical analysis of the wounds suffered came to the same kind of conclusions that had resulted in the reintroduction of steel helmets for infantry in 1915, namely that the majority of injuries were being caused by low-velocity shell fragments. As adding armor protection to the aircraft itself was out of the question, the only answer was to put body armor on the crews.

The man credited with beginning the development of this armor was Colonel Malcolm C. Grow, a surgeon of the Eighth Air Force. Grow began working with the Wilkinson Company of London in the fall of 1942. Wilkinson had been one of the manufacturers that had continued body armor production throughout the 1920s and '30s. Under Grow's direction they created a prototype body vest of overlapping 2-inch (13-cm) square steel plates sewn into padded canvas. The vest trialed in October and went into production as the Type A early in 1943, being first issued to crews of 12 B-17s in March.

At 16 lbs (7 kg) the Type A was heavy, and the men at first were unwilling to wear it on top of all their other flight gear. An education program was swiftly launched to counter this attitude, and throughout the squadrons the safety aspects of the vest were emphasized, including the red jettison tab on the front, which when pulled released all the fastenings holding front and back plates together.

The Type A was designed for use by the bombardier, navigator, radio operator, and the tail and waist gunners. There was no room for the armor in the upper and belly turrets. The pilot and co-pilot sat in armored seats and were not offered frontal armor protection until the arrival of the Type B half vest in 1943. Both types of body vest received additional groin armor – the Types C and D – in late 1943. A B-17 crewman was by now carrying up to 23 lbs (10 kilos) of armor.

The bomber crews were also issued with helmets. The first of these was the Type M3 of 1942, a leather-covered close-fitting armored helmet with areas left free over the ears for radio headphones. The M4 helmet followed this design but replaced the expensive leather covering with cheaper khaki drill. This pattern was superseded in its turn by the M4A2, which featured greater armor protection in the form of shaped plated flaps on each side of the crown, protecting the ears.

The final pattern of the war was the Type M5. Introduced in 1944, this was an all-steel modification of the Army's M1, and also featured separate plates hinged on each side to cover the ears and headphones. The helmet was covered in a paint and wool dust mix.

Toward the end of the war further developments included a high-collared neck armor (the T44) and a steel plate to cover the oxygen face mask, though neither of these items saw widespread service.

Just over 393,000 armored helmets of all types were issued to USAAF personnel from 1942 to 1945, together with 909,000 individual pieces of body armor. The effects were dramatic. Official reports concluded that from November 1943 to May 1944 wounds received by bomber crews fell by 61 percent.

Though proven in combat, the USAAF's armor program came to an end in 1945. The new generation of nuclear-armed strategic bombers – operated after 1947 by the US Air Force – would fly far beyond the range and targeting capabilities of any anti-aircraft gun, making the wearing of body armor by aircrew unneccesary. Armor development instead refocused back on the infantryman on the ground, and was to be given fresh impetus by the US Armys leading role in the Korean war, which broke out in June 1950.

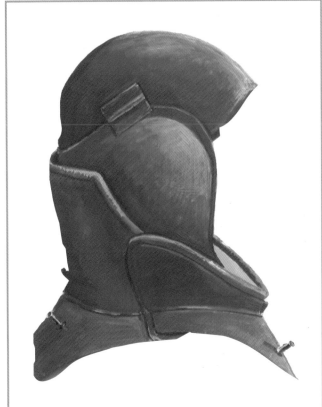

A B-17 flight crewman in full-armored rig. He wears the M3 steel helmet together with a Type B half vest and Type C groin armor. Inset: The USAAF's M5 steel helmet with the M13 pattern neck armor. The M5 was the final pattern of aircrew combat helmet produced before the war in Europe ended in 1945.

Right: The British "PH" gas helmet of January 1916. The cloth of the "helmet" was impregnated with chemicals to neutralize phosgene gas.

Far right: The British "small box" respirator of June 1916. This became the standard issue respirator of British forces until the end of the First World War. In 1918 proposals were made to turn the respirator haversack into a ballistic defense by inserting a steel plate.

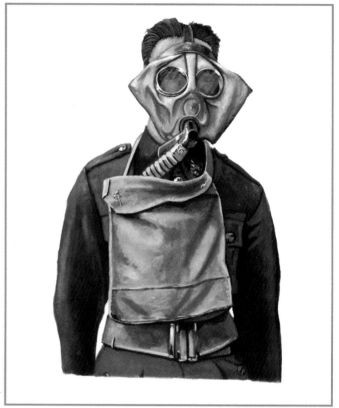

Right: The British box respirator of 1939. This pattern was replaced in 1943 by the Light Pattern Anti-Gas Respirator, which introduced a tubeless, single-filter canister design that is still in use at the beginning of the 21st century.

On the Western Front on 22 April 1915 the German Army discharged 150 tons of chlorine gas on an unsuspecting Algerian division in the French front line, and so began the modern history of chemical warfare. To defend troops against such an insidious form of attack, a completely new kind of personal defense was needed. This was not to be an armor against a physical blow but against deliberately planned chemical poisoning. The British were the first to respond to Germany's gas offensive in May 1915 with a simple mask respirator, which covered the nose and mouth. Full-face gas "helmets" were first introduced in the same year, and by June 1916 the "small box" respirator had been developed, of which over 13 million were produced by 1918.

The importance of gas protection to modern armor development lies in the fact that the combat armors of the 21st century will be both a ballistic defense and a proof against chemical, biological, and radiation poisoning.

The US Army's full Nuclear, Biological, Chemical warfare oversuit and respirator. This example is being worn with an M69 ballistic "flak" jacket. Unlike the British Army's No.1 Mk 4 NBC suit, this is not made in a disruptive camouflage material.

A police riot-control helmet of the late 1990s. Design features include a neck shield, movable vizor of impact-proof polycarbonate, and hearing apertures. Many riot helmets may also include a full communications setup of microphones and earpiece. The helmets of this type are usually able to provide a ballistic defense against .35 in (9mm) small arms ammunition.

1945 to the Present Day

The latter half of the 20th century would see body armor for the infantry soldier elevated from a specialized piece of equipment of rather dubious worth to a standard-issue item as essential as the combat helmet.

Credit for beginning this change lies, ironically, with the US Navy, which in 1943 began research into developing a lightweight armor for the Marine Corps and for its upper-deck personnel. The importance of the Navy's work was that for the first time a non-metallic substance would be considered as the ballistic material.

Companies in the United States, of course, already had experience of production processes using plastic and fiber in the production of the M1 helmet liner, and this technology was extended in 1943 with the development of "Doron," a glass-fiber and plastic multi-ply laminate, which in tests in 1945 was found to stop a .45 round at 800 ft/sec (244 m/sec). The "Doron" vest was first trialed with a Marine battalion during the invasion of Okinawa in April 1945.

The United States Ordnance Department also began to take a fresh interest in armor, and from 1944 began work on a fragmentation vest for the Army using aluminum and multi-ply nylon cloth. This culminated in August 1945 with the Armor Vest M12, weighing 12 lbs 3 oz (5.5 kg). Over 53,000 M12s were produced from June to August 1945.

In early 1951, faced with the urgent need for a fragmentation vest for US Marines then fighting in Korea, elements of both the M12 and the "Doron" vests were combined in a single design. The vest featured a nylon weave backing to overlapping "Doron" ballistic plates, which were positioned over the chest, back, and upper abdomen. This was a mixture of soft and hard armor types in one vest, a design widely adopted around the world in later decades in the so-called variable armors.

The new vest was trialed in combat and found to be extremely popular with front-line troops. A criticism that the vest became waterlogged in the wet and pounds heavier received prompt action with the introduction of a water-resistant cover. The vest went into full-scale production as the Vest, Armored,

An Israeli Defence Force "Rabintex" ballistic jacket of the early 1980s. Based on US Army designs such as the M69, the "Rabintex" was one of the first modern ballistic jackets to feature equipment pouches as an integral part of the design. Like the US "flak" jackets of the 1950s and '60s, however, it suffers from a design weakness in that it is secured by fasteners at the front of the body, the very area that needs the most protection. Armored vests produced in the late 1980s solved this problem by being secured at the sides.

The structure of the British GS Mk 6 combat helmet. Made of resin-impregnated ballistic nylon, the GS Mk 6 weighs 3 lb (1.35 kg) and can be converted for use in an internal security role by the fitting of a transparent vizor and neck guard. It is available in three sizes. Like the American PASGT helmet, the design includes space around both ears to allow the use of a radio headset.

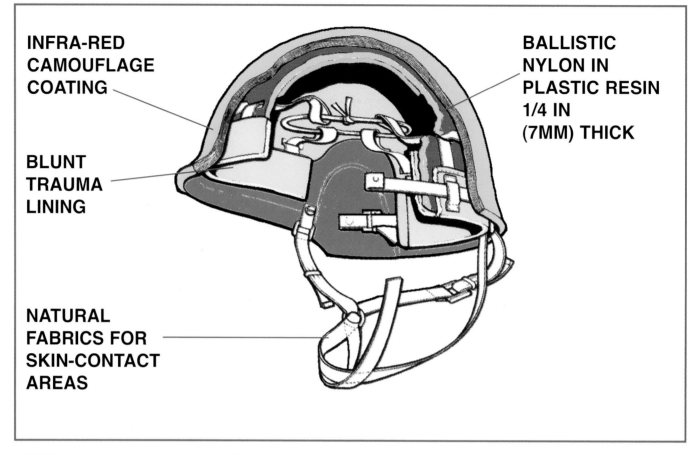

INFRA-RED CAMOUFLAGE COATING

BALLISTIC NYLON IN PLASTIC RESIN 1/4 IN (7MM) THICK

BLUNT TRAUMA LINING

NATURAL FABRICS FOR SKIN-CONTACT AREAS

M1951 and reached front-line Marine units by February 1952.

It was found that the M1951 reduced casualties by up to 30 percent. By March the 1st Marine Division had ordered 28,000 of the vests, and by July nearly 10,000 were in theater and operationally available.

The US Army were a little slower in providing fragmentation vests to its troops, trialing an all-nylon, foam-backed vest throughout March and July 1952. It was approved for service in October as the Armor Vest M1952, and 26,000 were in theater by the time of the Korean armistice of July 1953.

The success of the fragmentation jacket in Korea guaranteed its continued use as a standard-issue item in both the US Army and Marine Corps and both branches began development programs to upgrade and improve their own types.

The Marine Vest, Armored, M1955 featured a high ballistic collar of nylon, as did the Army's Body Armor Vest M69, which first appeared in 1962. As with their previous patterns of design, the Marine M1955 was a nylon and "Doron" composite, while the Army's M69 relied on close-weave nylon cloth – in this case up to 14-ply thick.

These four vest types were used throughout the Vietnam War, and from 1965 were joined by a series of hard ceramic plate armors developed for the protection of helicopter crews. These created the old problem of bullet disintegration on impact and in response a new pattern was introduced in 1968, which featured a ballistic nylon covering over the plates.

Both the Army and the Marines' "flak" jackets as they were popularly known, were worn in conjuction with the M1 helmet. This had seen no design upgrade to its steel outer shell since 1941, although in 1965 the inner liner began to be made from plastic laminated nylon.

The M1 was finally taken out of service in the late 1970s and replaced by the helmet of the US ground forces" Personnel Armor System Ground Troops

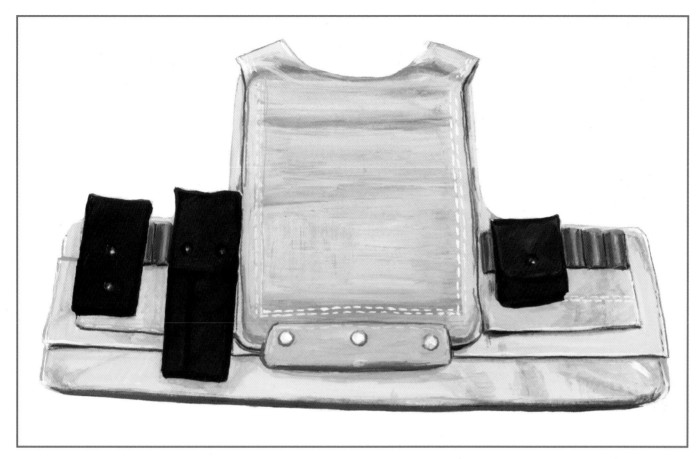

A "variable" armored vest of the late 1990s. This is a composite of both soft and hard types of armor protection. The "hard" ballistic plate of either ceramic or metal plate is secured over the front of the vest, which is made of closely woven multi-ply aramid fiber. The vest is secured at the sides and includes attachments for equipment pouches.

(PASGT) – introduced in 1976.

The PASGT helmet of Kevlar™ comes in a single size with an adjustable suspension system. It features some of the strongest features of earlier combat helmet design including the four-point chinstrap system. Its shape is also powerfully reminiscent of the M1935 stahlhelm, but critics of this were silenced when it was realized that for all its ugly connotations the M1935 remains one of the finest combat helmets ever produced.

This new helmet was designed to be worn in conjuction with the PASGT fragmentation vest. The vest has not, however, proved as successful as the helmet. Its original design was not proof against a 7.62 mm rifle bullet and as a result had to be worn with a later design addition, the Interim Small Arms Protective Overvest (ISAPO) which pushed the combined weight up to 25 lbs. (11 kg)

In Europe several NATO and former Warsaw Pact countries retained the use of steel combat helmets into the 1990s, usually where armies had a high proportion of conscripts, which made a change to new material uneconomic. This was not the case in Britain, where the GS Mk 6 was introduced in the late 1970s.

Made of ballistic nylon, the GS Mk 6 represents an important point of cross-over between modern armor used by a soldier for combat and that used by police organizations to maintain internal security.

The GS Mk 6 owes its development to the success of the Northern Ireland Combat Helmet, a glass-reinforced helmet with a four-point chinstrap and vizor attachment, developed by the British Army to replace the steel Mk IV, which was found to be obsolete in the face of the ever-worsening Troubles. Specific riot equipment also came out of the civil unrest including the first generation of ballistic riot helmets and clear plastic shields.

The need to counter terrorism with its indiscrimate use of explosive devices saw the creation of the Explosive Ordnance Disposal (EOD) suit. It is an

The most heavily armored of all present-day military personnel are those responsible for Explosive Ordnance Disposal (EOD). The EOD suit consists of both ballistic plates and aramid or UHMW fiber. It is designed to protect the disposal officer from the effects of blast, heat, over-pressure, and fragmentation. The latest designs under trial are also meant to protect against chemical and biological contamination. The helmet will include an integral radio set and breathing apparatus. Though of use in tackling smaller explosive devices, the EOD suit cannot protect against the largest.

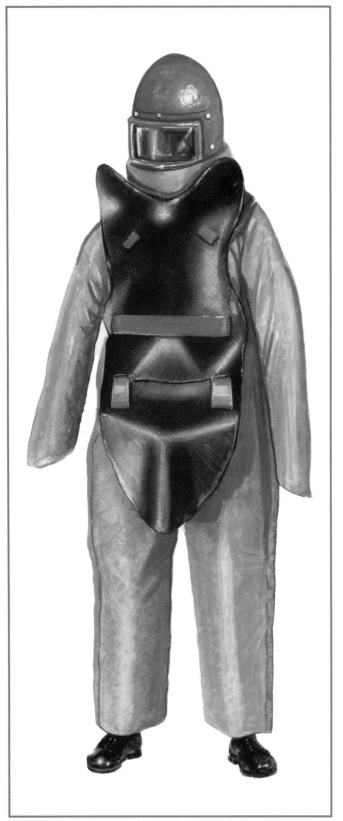

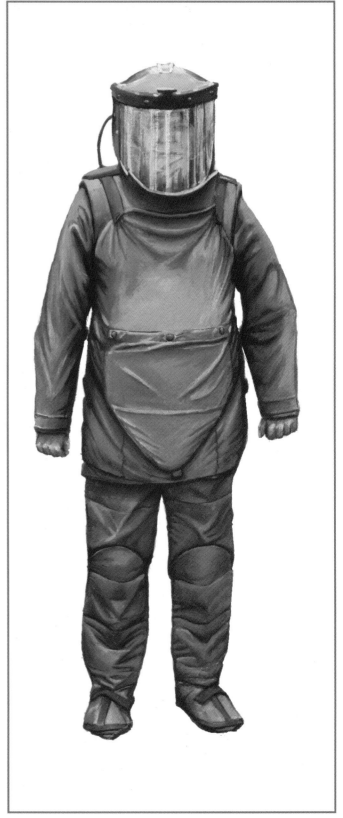

example of the most heavily armored form of body protection currently available. Bomb disposal personnel are provided with heavily vizored helmets and both hard and soft full body armor. The protection also includes radio communications equipment and may feature a ventilation system to protect against possible bio or chemical hazard fitted to the explosive. Also available to ordnance personnel are the more lightly armored Improvised Explosive Device (IED) suits, designed for routine searches in possible target areas.

The use of armor by internal security organisations expanded enormously in the last decades of the 20th century. Assault equipment for anti-terrorist or tactical police units around the world now uses the latest in synthetic materials to produce lightweight ballistic helmets and body armor comparable, if not superior, to the all-metal body defences of earlier centuries.

Helmets like the American PASGT are known as composite helmets, being made of aramid fiber (a form of nylon) such as Kevlar 129™, molded and impregnated with plastic resin for rigidity. The Kevlar™ provides a tensile strength per weight 5 times stonger than steel, creating a helmet weighing only 3.5 lbs (1.7 kg) capable of withstanding a .22 round at 2,000 f/ps. Kevlar™ is not the final word in synthetic materials for armor. The latest generation, developed in the 1980s, includes ultra-high molecular weight (UHMW) polyethylene fibers such Spectra™, which have a per-weight strength ten times that of steel.

The helmets may include the earphones and microphone of a fully integrated communications system, and can be configured to act as an equipment platform for night-vision equipment. Most helmets are designed to be worn with both a gas respirator and a full-face clear plastic ballistic vizor, the vizor giving protection to the face up to at least National Institute of Justice (NIJ) Standard Level IIA. (For explanations of the NIJ Standards and equivalents in Europe and Russia, please see Appendix, page 152).

If neither vizor or respirator is being worn then personnel wear goggles, made to the same protective standard as the full vizor. Also available is a full-face armored mask of Kevlar™ made by the American

The US Army"s PASGT combat helmet and fragmentation jacket at the time of the Gulf War, 1990-91. In contrast to the PASGT helmet, which has proved a success since its first operational use in Grenada in 1983, the fragmention jacket has now had to be replaced by the Interceptor Body Armor System, which is a lighter, modular, variable armor using both ballistic fiber and ceramic plates.

Inserting a ballistic plate into the front of a "variable" armored vest. A similar plate could also be inserted in the back. Ballistic plates can be made from a variety of materials: aramid and nylon fibers in plastic resin or metal surrounded by ceramic or glass fiber. Each plate should weigh no more than 4 lbs 6 oz (2 kg)

One of the growth areas in armor design is the so-called "concealed" vest. Originally for the use of those involved in personal protection and security, these covert armors are finding a new role among military peace-keepers, in situations where standard-issue military "flak" jackets might be seen as threatening by civilian populations.

Body Armor Equipment, Inc. Visually the scariest of modern armors — looking like a hockey mask - it is in use with the Italian NOCs tactical police unit.

The armored vest is of the variable type, essentially a piece of soft armor consisting of dense layers of woven aramid fiber. The vest is quite capable of stopping a 9 mm Parabellum round but is insufficient against a 7.62 mm rifle bullet. To counter this threat the vest has large pockets in both front and back into which separate ballistic plates can be inserted.

The plates come in three basic forms: metal, such as titanium or tungsten; a mosaic of small ceramic tiles; and a single plate of ceramic known as a "monolithic." The plates are backed with either glass fiber or aramid fiber. The aramid backing is considered superior, as — unlike glass fibre — it does not fracture on impact, allowing the plate to be reused.

Armored vests of the higher quality will have a "blunt trauma layer" in the inner lining. Usually consisting of UHMW fiber, this trauma shield is designed to absorb and dissipate the kinetic energy of a bullet and prevent impact damage to bones or internal organs.

Additions to the basic vest can include a separate plate to protect the groin and a high ballistic collar. Many of the latest vests now feature high collars as standard. None of these additions, however, should restrict the wearer"s ease of movement, one of the primary considerations in an armor"s design. In total a body armor with ballistic plates offering protection up to NIJ Level IIIA should weigh no more than 9-11 lbs (4-5 kg).

The vest is secured to the body at the sides using self-adhesive Velcro™ straps or plastic clips; metal fastenings are kept to an absolute minimum to reduce the threat posed to the wearer by the metal under impact. Velcro™ is also used to secure items such as communications equipment and pouches directly onto the armor, although load-carrying tactical vests are usually worn on top if the amount of equipment to be carried is too great. These tactical vests are made ideally of a light nylon mesh to save weight.

Personnel on operations may also wear knee and elbow protectors of reinforced plastic, though these are mainly for impact protection rather than ballistic defense.

All armored vests are covered in a flame-and-solvent resistant material. The color is invariably black or dark blue for urban operations, although some SWAT (Special Weapons and Tactics) teams in states such as Arizona wear their armor in a standard Army camouflage pattern.

Police tactical teams may also carry ballistic shields. Not to be confused with riot shields, these are made of Kevlar, UHMW, and ceramics and can provide ballistic protection up to NIJ Level IV (a 30-caliber AP round at over 2,820 ft/sec 860 m/s). Ballistic shields come in a variety of sizes and configurations to counter increasing levels of threat. The smallest, at 17 x 23 in (45 x 60 cm) and weighing 9 lbs (4 kg) can be held on the arm and provide protection against 9 mm pistol fire in enclosed spaces such as stairwells and doorways. The largest offering protection against rifle fire and grenade blasts are equipped with wheels, clear ballistic polycarbonate viewing panels, and battery-powered spotlights. These can weigh from 66 to 156 lbs (30 kg to 71 kg) and measure up to 3 x 5 ft (1 x 1.5 m).

In this age of terrorists and armed criminals, there are also hand-held ballistic mini-shields. These take the form of clipboards for use at checkpoints and weigh about 2 lbs 5 oz (just over 1 kg).

In some police forces in the world, as well as among officers in prisons and other correctional facilities, the main threat to life comes not from a bullet but from a knife. To counter this, anti-knife vests were developed in the 1980s, primarily in Britain. Both concealable inner and outer vests are commercially available. The inner vest is designed to be worn under a uniform and is made of Kevlar™, though this provides only a backing for lightweight jointed metal plates (often of titanium) front and rear. The inner vests weighs approximately 5 lbs 8oz (2.5 kg). An outer anti-stab vest has recently been developed by First Defense International in the United States. It weighs approximately 8 lbs (3.5 kg) and features a high protective collar and single release buckle. Both vests provide full torso protection (they do not leave unguarded gaps between the front and back plate for an attack from the side), but neither provides a ballistic defense. In recognition of their widespread use, special standards have been introduced by authorities both in Britain and the United States to test

A special forces assault equipment of the early 1980s. The armor is secured with plastic fastenings and Velcro™; this keeps potentially hazardous metal fastenings to a minimum. The use of Velcro™ also allows communications equipment to be secured directly onto the vest. The overalls, gloves, and boots would be treated with flame-resistant chemicals.

A diagram of the structure of the assault armor seen on page 145. The vest consists of three separate layers manufactured from three different materials: a ceramic, an aramid fiber, and finally a blunt trauma layer, probably made from a dense UHMW material. The whole vest would be covered in flame-resistant material and to be practical would weigh no more than 14 lbs (6 kg).

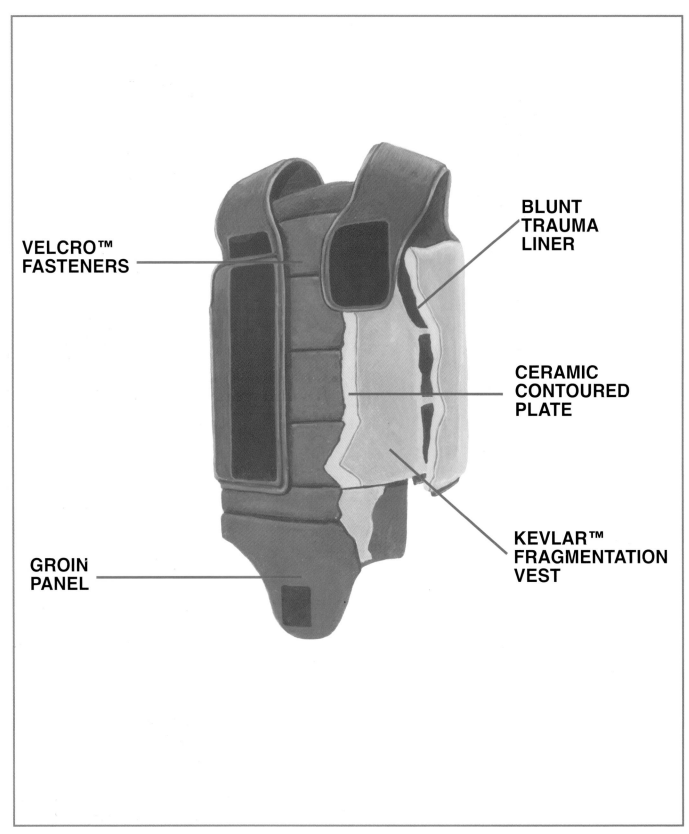

VELCRO™ FASTENERS

BLUNT TRAUMA LINER

CERAMIC CONTOURED PLATE

KEVLAR™ FRAGMENTATION VEST

GROIN PANEL

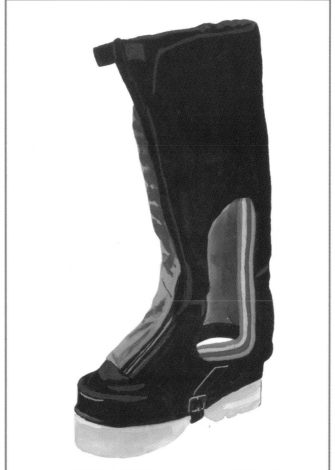

A blast gaiter used in the TFL Countermine protective system. An inner and outer boot are worn, together with this gaiter made of Kevlar™. The object is to deflect and absorb blast, heat, and fragments from the detonating mine. Injury to the foot and leg can be minimized by wearing such equipment, but can never be avoided altogether. The design of these new kinds of armored footwear is influenced by high-tech ski and climbing boots.

Above: The threat posed by millions of anti-personnel mines around the world in the last decades of the 20th century has created the necessity for an entirely new kind of body armor to be developed. The protection of the feet and lower legs has never been a high priority among armorers, but now the need to protect individuals against mines, particularly during the disposal of these weapons, has created the armored blast-proof boot.

Left: Though millions of mines were laid during the Second World War, there was no development of protective garments or equipment for those personnel responsible for removing them. This improvised get-up by a British Army soldier in 1944-45 may look efficient enough, but you have to wonder how he would actually kneel down to clear the mine once it was found.

Shields, like other forms of body armor, made a comeback in the 20th century. From the 1970s onwards internal security and riot control created a market for lightweight anti-impact shields that is now worldwide. Police forces use a wide variety of types.

Right is shown a round plastic riot shield used by British police. It weighs approximately 3 lbs (1.4 kg) and is made of the same hardened plastic as that used in the helmet vizor.

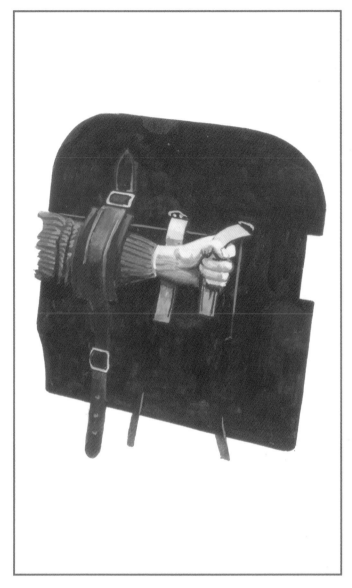

The British Army's experience of riots on the streets of Northern Ireland in the early 1970s went a long way to help develop riot-control equipment, which has since become standard. The clear plastic shield weighing approximately 9 lb 4 oz (4.5 kg) was introduced in the mid-1970s. The vizored "GRP" riot-control helmet was issued at the same time, after it was realized that the Mk IV steel combat helmet (the same pattern as the Mk III of 1944) gave insufficient protection from this new form of threat.

Police armed assault units such the SWAT (Special Weapons and Tactics) teams in the United States also use ballistic shields. Not to be confused with riot-control shields, they are often made from aramid fiber and ceramic and can provide ballistic protection from ammunition ranging from 9 mm revolver to a 7.62 mm full-metal-jacketed round. This particular example is ideal for use in enclosed spaces such as aircraft doorways or stairwells. Larger examples are full-body length and can be provided with wheels, battery-powered lights, and viewing panels of a clear ballistic polycarbonate.

the stab-resistance of this type of protective armor (see Appendix).

Other specialist forms of armor created from the 1980s onwards include ballistic vests designed specifically for women, in response to their growing numbers in the military and law enforcement, and ballistic flotation vests. These are aimed at the customs service and coastguard market and combine full buoyancy with protection up to NIJ Levels III and IV. They can also be fitted with a range of maritime extras such as flashing rescue lights and radio beacons.

So-called executive vests have also seen a growth in popularity, particularly in the Russian Federation. These provide lightweight covert protection for businessmen, diplomats, and personal security personnel. Designed to fit under outer clothing or even disguised as a suit vest, these armors provide stab protection and a limited ballistic defense against .35 in (9 mm) ammunition at 1,033 ft/sec (315 m/sec).

The new generation of armors developed through the last years of the 1990s continue this trend towards specialization in design and purpose. Advances in materials science and the economies created by a global market have meant that armors can now be created or adapted to counter a specific threat in a specific environment. No longer will one "flak" jacket be relied upon in every threatening environment from urban riot to jungle battlefield.

In October 1999 the US Army introduced its latest type of protective armor system. Known as Interceptor Body Armor (IBA) it will replace the PASGT vest and ISAPO. At 16 lbs 1 oz (7.3 kg) it is over 8 lbs (about 3.5 kg) lighter and has been designed as a modular system that can be adapted to cope with changing levels of threat from peace-keeping to combat operations. While the PASGT was originally developed as a fragmentation vest only, the IBA is a variable armor with pockets for ballistic plates front and back, plus a detachable collar and groin plate. It was trialed with both the Army and Marine Corps and will serve with both branches.

The needs of international peace-keeping have also led to trials at the US Army Soldier Systems Center (Natick) of a concealable ballistic armor for military police. The vest is variable and is aimed to provide protection against 0.3 in (7.62 mm) rifle ammunition. With ballistic plates inserted it is likely to weigh about 19 lbs 13 oz (9 kg). A version for female personnel will also be produced.

The danger posed around the world by anti-personnel mines has also produced a response by armor manufacturers. Both commercial companies and the US military have invested heavily in creating new forms of foot and leg armor to protect against blast and fragmentation. This is the first time such an armor has ever been considered.

The US Body Armor Set, Individual Countermine (BASIC) system, features a ballistic layered over-trouser, while on the feet an over-boot (much like a ski-boot in appearance) fits over the soldier's combat boot. Made of nylon, the over-boot has a composite plastic and aluminum sole. In the commercial market, companies such as TFL Countermine in Britain have created an anti-mine boot comprising three separate levels of protection. An insulated inner liner fits into a modified plastic climbing boot strengthened on the sole with layers of UHMW materials, over which goes an outer gaiter of Kevlar™ and ballistic nylon that comes up to the knee.

The use of armor today is more widespread than it has ever been, and the future promises evermore sophisticated methods of body protection. Advances in materials technology create the possibility of "smart" textiles, which can alter their own molecular structure to counter changing ballistic or NBC threats, while the combat helmet, according to some visionaries, will be by 2025 a fully integrated communications and tactical system linked directly to a command and control center.

If these projections are science fiction, they are only a little short of science fact. The history of armor has always been driven by the practical need to counter new kinds of physical danger, created, very often, from new forms of conflict and type of weapon. It will be from the needs of the man or woman under threat that body armor will take its new forms in the future. As it has always been.

An American riot cop stands guard at the end of the 20th century. American police were first issued with Kevlar™ vests in 1975, and some would say that this Seattle officer is the ultimate expression of the armored policeman. But looks can be deceptive; although he is intimidating to look at, his armor is made of foam-padded blocks and is designed to protect against blows not bullets. What is more, his helmet does not have any form of neck shield, a surprising omission since most riot helmets today can be fitted with them.

APPENDIX: BALLISTIC TESTS

Ballistic tests depend on many variables including the composition, mass, shape, velocity, and caliber of the round fired.

The US National Institute of Justice (NIJ) 0101.03 Standard for Ballistic Resistance was introduced in 1987. In October 2000 this was superseded by the new 0101.04 Standard.

US NATIONAL INSTITUTE OF JUSTICE (NIJ) STANDARD 0101.03 (DETAIL)

Level	Ammunition caliber	Velocity m/s	Max trauma (mm)
1	.22 lead	320	44
11	.375 Magnum soft point 9 mm metal jacket	425-440 358-373	44
111	7.62 mm metal jacket	838-853	44
111A	.44 Magnum soft conical 9 mm metal jacket	426-441 426-441	44
1V	30-06 AP	868-883	44

COMMITTEE EUROPEAN NORMALIZATION BODY ARMOR STANDARD

Level	Ammunition caliber	Velocity m/s
BR 1	.32 round nose	300
BR 2	9 mm soft lead core	400
BR 3	.357 conical	430
BR 4	.44 flat nose	440
BR 5	5.56 rifle	950
BR 6	7.63 rifle	830
BR 7	7.62 rifle hard core	820

RUSSIAN STATE BALLISTIC STANDARD

Level	Ammunition caliber	Velocity m/sec
1	9 mm 7.62 revolver	290-315
2	5.45 mm pistol 7.62 pistol	310-325 415-445
3	5.45 mm (AK-74) 7.62 mm (AKM)	870-890 710-725
4	7.62 mm sniper	820-835

UK POLICE SCIENTIFIC DEVELOPMENT BRANCH STAB-RESISTANT STANDARD 1999

Level	Energy Level E1 (joules)	Max Penetration (mm)	Energy Level E 2 (joules)	Max Penetration (mm)
KR1	24	7	36	20
KR2	33	7	50	20
KR3	43	7	65	20

BIBLIOGRAPHY

This is a general bibliography, which includes books the authors found helpful. Although it is by no means exhaustive, many of the titles listed include more extensive bibliographies, which will take the interested reader deeper into his or her own areas of interest.

A

Anderson, JL, *Japanese Armour*, London, 1968.

Arnold, C, Steelpots: *A History of Americas Steel Combat Helmets*, San Jose, 1997.

B

Baer, L, Dahl, K. Daniel (trans), *The History of the German Steel Helmet, 1916-1945*, San Jose 1985.

Barber, R, & Barker, J, *Tournaments*, Woodbridge, 1989.

Barker, AJ, *Japanese Army Handbook, 1939-45*, London, 1979.

Barthorp, M, *British Cavalry Uniforms Since 1660*, London, 1984.

Benitez-Johannot, P, & Barbier, JP, *Boucliers d'Afrique, d'Asie du Sud-Est et d'Oceanie*, Paris, 1998.

Blackmore, D, *Arms and Armour of the English Civil Wars*, London, 1990.

Blackmore, HL, *Arms and Armour*, London, 1965.

Blair, C, *European Armour circa 1066 to circa 1700*, London, 1979.

Boccia, LG, & Coelho, ET, *L'Arte dell'Armatura in Italia*, Milan, 1967.

Boccia, LG, *Le Armatura di S. Maria delle Grazia di Curtatone di Mantova e l'Armatura Lombarda del' 400*, Busto Arizio, 1982.

Bottomley, I, & Hopson, AP, *Arms & Armour of the Samurai*, London, 1996.

C

Caldwell, DH, *The Scottish Armoury*, Edinburgh, 1979.

Caldwell, DH, *Scottish Weapons and Fortifications, 1100-1800*, Edinburgh, 1981.

Clephan, RC, *The Tournament: its Periods and Phases*, London, 1919.

Coggins, J, *Arms and Equipment of the Civil War*, New York, 1962

Connolly, P, *Greece and Rome at War*, London, 1981.

Cripps Day, FH, *The Tournament in England and France*, London, 1918.

Cripps Day, FH, *A Record of Armour Sales, 1881- 1924*, London, 1925.

Curtis, HM, *2,500 Years of European Helmets 800 BC-1700 AD*, North Hollywood, 1978.

D

Davis, BL, *British Army Uniforms and Insignia of World War Two*, London, 1983.

Davis, BL, *German Army Uniforms and Insignia of World War Two*, London, 1998.

Dean, Bashford, *Helmets and Body Armor in Modern Warfare*, New Haven, 1920.

Dufty, A, *European Armour in the Tower of London*, London, 1968.

Dunn, Capt. JC, *The War the Infantry Knew 1914-1919*, London, 1987.

E

Edge, D, & Paddock, JM, *Arms and Armour of the Medieval Knight*, London, 1988.

Egerton of Tatton, Lord W, *Description of Indian and Oriental Armour*, London, 1896.

Elgood, R (ed.), *Islamic Arms and Armour*, London, 1977.

F

ffoulkes, CJ, *The Armourer and his Craft*, London, 1912.

G

Gamber, O (ed.), *Glossarium Armorum: Arma Defensiva*, Graz, 1972-1999.

Gamber, O, *Waffe und Rüstung Eurasiens*, Braunschweig, 1978.

Gay, V, *Glossaire Archologique du Moyen Age et de la Renaissance*, 2 Vols, Paris, 1887 and 1928.

Grant, M, *Gladiators*, London, 1971.

H

Haythornwaite, P, *Weapons and Equipment of the Napoleonic Wars*, Dorset, 1979.

Hayward, JF, *European Armour*, London, 1965.

Hencken, H, *The Earliest European Helmets*, Cambridge (Mass.), 1971.

Holmes, MR, *Arms & Armour in Tudor & Stuart London*, London, 1970.

J

Johnson, D, *The French Cavalry 1792-1815*, London, 1989.

K

Karcheski, WJ, *Arms and Armor of the Conquistador, 1492-1600*, Miami, 1990.

L

Laking, Sir GF, *A Record of European Armour and Arms*, 5 Vols, 1920-22 (Reprinted 2000).

Lindesay, W, *The Terracotta Army of the First Emperor of China*, Hong Kong, 1998.

M

Martin, P, *Armour and Weapons*, London, 1968.

Miller, Y, (ed.) *Russian Arms and Armour*, Leningrad, 1982.

Muller, H, *Alte Helme*, Berlin, 1979.

Muller, H, & Kunter, F, *Europäische Helme*, Berlin, 1982.

N

Nickel, H, *Arms and Armor in Africa*, New York, 1971.

Nickel, H, *Arms and Armour through the Ages*, London, 1971.

Nicolle, D, *Arms & Armour of the Crusading Era 1050-1350*, 2 Vols, London, 1999.

Norman, AVB, *Arms and Armour*, London, 1964.

Norman, AVB, & Pottinger, D, *Warrior to Soldier 449-1660*, London, 1966.

Norris, J, & Fowler, W, *NBC*, London, 1997.

O

Oakeshott, RE, *The Archaeology of Weapons: Arms and Armour from Prehistory to the Age of Chivalry*, London, 1960.

Oakeshott, RE, *A Knight and his Armour*, London, 1961.

Oakeshott, RE, *European Weapons and Armour from the Renaissance to the Industrial Revolution*, Guildford, 1980.

P

Peterson, HL, *A History of Body Armor*, New York, 1968.

Peterson, HL, *Arms and Armor in Colonial America, 1526-1783*, New York, 1956.

Pfaffenbichler, M, *Medieval Craftsmen; Armourers*, London, 1992.

Pyhrr, S, *European Helmets, 1450-1650*, New York, 2000.

Pyhrr, S, *Heroic Armor of the Italian Renaissance*, New York, 1998.

R

Rangstrom, L, *Riddarlek och Tornerspel (Tournaments and the Dream of Chivalry)*, Stockholm, 1992.

Rankin, Colonel RH, *Military Headdress*, London, 1976.

Reid, W, *The Lore of Arms*, London, 1976.

Richardson, T, & Karcheski, WJ, *The Medieval Armour from Rhodes*, Leeds, 2000.

Robinson, HR, *The Armour of Imperial Rome*, London, 1976.

Robinson, HR, *Armours of Henry VIII*, London, 1977.

Robinson, HR, *Oriental Armour*, London, 1967.

Robinson, HR, *Japanese Arms and Armour*, London, 1969.

Robinson, HR, *A Short History of Japanese Armour*, London, 1965.

S

Snodgrass, AM, *Arms and Armour of the Greeks*, London, 1967.

Snodgrass, AM, Early *Greek Armour and Weapons, from the end of the Bronze Age to 600 BC*, Edinburgh, 1964.

Spring, C, *African Arms and Armour*, London, 1993.

Stephenson, IP, *Roman Infantry Equipment, The Later Empire*, Stroud, 1999.

Stone, GC, *A Glossary of the Construction, Decoration, and Use of Arms and Armor in All Countries and in All Times*, New York, 1934.

Sweeting, CG, *Combat Flying Equipment: 1917-45*, Shrewsbury, 1989.

T

Tarassuk, L, & Blair, C (eds), *The Complete Encyclopaedia of Arms and Weapons*, London, 1982.

Thomas, B, and Gamber, O, *Die Innsbrucker Plattnerkunst (Catalogue)*, Innsbruck, 1954.

Trapp, O, & Mann, Sir JG, *Catalogue of the Armoury at the Castle of Churburg*, London, 1929.

Tweddle, D, *The Anglian Helmet from Coppergate*, York, 1992.

U

Underwood, R, *Anglo-Saxon Weapons & Warfare*, Stroud, 1999.

V

Viollet-le-Duc, EE, *Dictionnaire du mobilier francais de l'époque carlovingienne à la Renaissance (Vols V and VI, Armes de guerre offensives et defensives)*, Paris, 1874.

W

Wagner, E, *Medieval Costume, Armour, and Weapons, 1350-1450*, London, 1962.

Waterer, JW, *Leather and the Warrior*, Northampton, 1981.

Wenli, Z, *The Qin Terracotta Army*, London, 1996.

Wilkinson, F, *Battle Dress*, London, 1970.

Wilkinson, F, *Arms and Armour*, London, 1978.

Williams, A, & de Reuck, A, *The Royal Armoury at Greenwich 1515-1649*, London, 1995.

Wirgin, J, *The Emperor's Warriors*, Edinburgh, 1985.

Y

Yadin, Y, *The Art of Warfare in Biblical Lands*, London, 1963.

Young, A, *Tudor and Jacobean Tournaments*, London, 1987.

Excellent articles on individual aspects of armor have appeared in the following journals:

Journal of the Arms and Armour Society, London, 1953- ongoing (which includes listings of recent publications).

Livrustkammaren, Journal of the Royal Armoury, Stockholm, 1937- ongoing.

Royal Armouries Yearbook, Leeds, 1996- ongoing.

Waffen-und Kostümkunde, Germany, 1959- ongoing.

INDEX

WHERE TO SEE ARMOR

This listing is a brief guide to major collections of international importance. Museums are constantly changing and developing institutions and some collections may not always be on display, for a number of reasons. Public access to any collections held in reserve should be possible if prior arrangements are made. To find the addresses and current telephone numbers please consult the most recent edition of *The World of Learning*.

Austria
Graz (Landeszeughaus)
Ingoldstadt (Bayerisches Armeemuseum)
Vienna
(Kunsthistoriches Museum; Historiches Museum der Stadt Wien)

Belgium
Brussels (Musée Royal de l'Armée et d'Histoire Militaire)
Liège (Musée d'Armes)

Canada
Toronto (Royal Ontario Museum)

China
Lintong (Terracotta Army Museum)

Denmark
Copenhagen (Tojhusmuseet)

England
Cambridge (Fitzwilliam Museum)
Leeds (Royal Armouries Museum)
London (British Museum; HM Tower of London;
Victoria and Albert Museum; The Wallace Collection)
Windsor (The Castle)

France
Paris (Musée de l'Armée)

Germany
Dresden (Armeemuseum; Historisches Museum)
Munich (Bayerisches National Museum)
Nuremberg (The Castle)

Greece
Athens (National Archaeological Museum)

Italy
Churburg (Schloss Churburg)
Florence (Bargello; Museo Stibbert)
Turin (Armeria Reale)

Venice (Palazzo Ducale)

Japan
Tokyo (National Museum)

Netherlands
Amsterdam (Rijksmuseum)
Delft (Nederlands Leger en Wapenmuseum)

Russia
Moscow (Kremlin)
St. Petersburg (State Hermitage)

Scotland
Edinburgh (Royal Museums of Scotland)
Glasgow (Art Gallery and Museum)
Kilmarnock (Dean Castle)

Spain
Madrid (Armeria Real; Museo del Ejercito)

Sweden
Skokloster (The Castle)
Stockholm (Livrustkammaren; Statens Historiska Museet)

Switzerland
Basel (Historisches Museum)
Bern (Historisches Museum)
Geneva (Musée d'Art et d'Histoire)
Zurich (Schweizerisches Landesmuseum)

United States of America
Chicago (The Art Institute of Chicago)
Cleveland (Museum of Art)
New York (Metropolitan Museum of Art)
Philadelphia (Kienbusch Collection)
Washington (The Smithsonian Institution)
Worcester (The Higgins Armory Museum)